King Snakes As Pets.

King Snakes Comprehensive Owner's Guide.

King Snakes care, costs, feeding, cages, heating, lighting and health all included.

by

Marvin Murkett and Ben Team

GW00684862

Table of Contents

Table of Contents

Table of Contents

About The Authors

Marvin Murkett is an experienced writer and a true animal lover. He has been keeping reptiles and amphibians for over 30 years. He enjoys writing animal books and advising others how to take care of their animals to give them a happy home.

Ben Team is an environmental educator and author with over 16 years of professional reptile-keeping experience.

Ben currently maintains www.FootstepsInTheForest.com, where he shares information, narration and observations of the flora, fauna and habitats of Metro Atlanta.

While he thoroughly enjoys writing about the natural world, Ben's favorite moments are those spent in the company of his beautiful wife.

Foreword

The fear of snakes is common to people all over the world, and many would prefer to avoid encounters with snakes altogether. However, even the most dedicated ophidiophobe is likely to have a soft spot for kingsnakes – the infamous snakes that kill other snakes.

Known for being immune to the venom of rattlesnakes, cottonmouths and copperheads, kingsnakes appear as allies to humans in the battle against these potentially dangerous animals. Even those inclined to dispatch each and every snake they encounter are likely to permit kingsnakes to prowl in peace.

While this snake-killing reputation is well deserved, kingsnakes are not as benevolent as many have come to believe they are. Kingsnakes do not kill rattlesnakes as part of a desire to help protect humanity – they kill other snakes because they are *prey*.

They do not specifically seek out venomous species either; kingsnakes will eat a garter snake just as readily as a rattlesnake. However, as the consumption of garter snakes does not seem fantastic or beneficial, such details fail to spread through human culture.

In truth, most kingsnakes are as content consuming rodents, lizards or birds, as they are snakes. They are opportunistic hunters, happy to dine on virtually any small animal that they encounter.

In addition to being popular among the general public, kingsnakes have become incredibly popular in the reptile hobby. Kingsnakes are one of the most widely bred reptiles, and pet stores, websites and pet expos overflow with young serpents for sale.

This is an important development, as many kingsnakes are declining or rare in the wild. Others inhabit areas that are not safe or feasible for herpetologists to study. For example, many of the Central American and Mexican species are very poorly known – it would be tragic if they disappeared before scientists were able to document and study them thoroughly.

These population declines are not restricted to developing countries. Eastern kingsnakes are becoming increasingly rare in the southeastern United States, while some kingsnakes of the Western United States have already experienced drastic population declines. (David A. Steen1, 2010) (CHRISTOPHER T. WINNE, 2007)

Most of these population declines are the result of habitat destruction. Collection for the pet trade is also a factor, but the success of captive breeding programs has made the collection of wild kingsnakes an economically unviable activity.

The disappearance of kingsnakes is a serious problem. Kingsnakes are very important predators and prey in the ecosystems in which they live; without them, the habitats are sure to suffer.

However, with robust captive populations and increased societal awareness of the high cost of habitat destruction, these snakes may be saved before they disappear completely.

While captive populations provide some protection against complete extinction, these snakes are many generations removed from their wild ancestors and unsuitable for release back into the wild. Nevertheless, it is better to have a species thriving in captivity, than nowhere at all.

Fortunately for those interested in snakes, one of the best ways to build support for habitat protection and end the senseless killing of snakes is to expose people to snakes – particularly kingsnakes – in a positive and responsible manner.

Chapter 1: Anatomy and Basic Biology

While the term "kingsnake" applies to many different species, which exhibit great diversity, they all share a number of physical, anatomical and behavioral similarities. All forms have smooth scales, kill their prey by constriction and tend to be secretive in nature.

Physically, the different species have varying body proportions, sizes, colors and patterns, but all possess broadly similar internal anatomy that is typical for medium-sized colubrid snakes.

Tongue, Nose and Vomeronasal Organ

The forked tongue of snakes is one of their most famous characteristics. The forked tongue is a sensory organ that is not used in feeding or sound production.

The tongue is extended from the mouth to collect volatile particles from the environment. Then, when the tongue is withdrawn, it transfers these particles to the vomeronasal organ. The vomeronasal organ functions as an additional sense of smell or taste.

The vomeronasal organ (located in the roof of the mouth), has two openings – one for each tip of the snake's tongue. This allows snakes to process directional information picked up by the tongue. Snakes also use their nostrils to detect airborne chemicals in the environment.

Eyes

Kingsnakes have eyes that are fairly typical by snake standards. As a prowling, rather than ambushing, group of snakes, they have round pupils (F. BRISCHOUX†, 2010). Most kingsnakes see

9

movement well, but as with most snakes, their vision is relatively poor.

Most kingsnakes have golden-brown irises. Grey-banded kingsnakes (*Lampropeltis alterna*) have grey irises, while the iris of Mexican black kings (*Lampropeltis nigritus*), black kings (*Lampropeltis nigra*) and black milks (*Lampropeltis gaigeae*) are very dark.

Snakes lack moveable eyelids, meaning that their eyes are open at all times – even while they sleep. In fact, it can be difficult (or impossible) to tell whether a motionless snake is sleeping or awake.

To protect their eye, snakes have a clear scale, called the spectacle. Like all other scales on the snake's body, they shed them periodically.

Ears

Snakes lack external ears, but they do have rudimentary middle and inner ears. Part of the reason for this is that the bones which normal reside in the ears of mammals have moved to the jaws of snakes. They now serve as the quadrate bone!

Accordingly, snakes hear very little if at all. Scientists debate the finer points of their abilities, but suffice to say, snakes do not come when called. Nor do they appear to respond to most airborne sounds. However, snakes can feel very low frequency vibrations through the substrate, such as footsteps.

Scales

The outer covering of a snake's body is comprised of scales. Scales are modified pieces of skin that form in regular rows along the snake's body. Between these scales, the skin is soft and flexible, which allows snakes to stretch to accommodate food items or eggs.

Some snakes have scales that feature a ridge down the center of each scale, while others – including all kingsnakes – have smooth, scales. Scales that feature such ridges are said to be keeled.

Noting the presence of absence of keels can be helpful in identifying unknown snakes. For example, one of the easiest ways to distinguish a black kingsnake (*Lampropeltis nigra*) from an eastern rat snake (*Pantherophis alleghaniensis*) is by noting the scales. Black kingsnakes have smooth scales, while rat snakes have keeled scales.

Tail

While they look like heads that seamlessly transition into tails, the tails of snakes are shorter than most people realize. The tail starts at the vent (where the hipbones would be if kingsnakes had them) and travel to the end of the body. Kingsnakes do not have much gripping strength in their tails, but they are capable of vibrating them to dissuade predators. Additionally, some snakes thrash their tails while musking to help spray a greater area with the foul-smelling liquid.

Wild snakes frequently show signs of healed tail injuries.

Vent

The vent is the place from which snakes defecate and release urates. Additionally, it is the exit point for their reproductive organs and eggs or young. Inside the vent lies a chamber called the cloaca, which holds these products until they are expelled through the vent.

Skeletal System

Aside from the details of the skull, and the lack of an appendicular skeleton (pelvic girdles, hip girdles and their accompanying limb bones), the snake's skeleton is quite similar to that of other vertebrates.

Snakes have elongated bodies, so they have many more vertebrae than humans or cows, for example. Each vertebrae attaches to two rib bones. The degree of flexibility between each vertebrae is much greater in constricting snakes, such as kingsnakes, than it is in most other animals.

Unlike the helmet-like skull of mammals, the skull of snakes is a loosely articulated collection of strut- and plate-like bones. This allows them to open their mouth wide enough to eat large prey.

Six different bones in the snake's skull hold teeth, which are arranged in the mouth in four rows. Two rows of teeth sit along the perimeter of the top and bottom jaw, while two others form parallel rows of teeth in the roof of the snake's mouth.

Contrary to popular perception, snakes do not dislocate their jaws when swallowing prey. They simply possess more complex joints than humans do. Instead of the mandible connecting directly to the skull (as occurs in humans and most other vertebrates), the mandible of snakes connects to the quadrate bone. The quadrate bone, in turn, connects to the skull. This arrangement allows the quadrate bone to swing down and forward, while the mandible pivots downward and forward as well. This produces a far larger gape than any similar sized animal has.

Internal Organs

Snakes have internal organs that largely mirror those of other vertebrates, with a few exceptions.

The digestive system of snakes is relatively similar to those of other animals, featuring an esophagus that accepts food from the mouth and transports it to the stomach, and long intestines that transport food from the stomach to the anus where the food residue is expelled. Along the way, the liver, gall bladder and pancreas aid the digestive process.

Snakes propel blood through their bodies via a heart and circulatory system. One important difference lies in their pulmonary anatomy – advanced snakes (such as kingsnakes) feature only one fully functional lung.

The kidneys of snakes are paired as they are in most other animals, but they have a staggered alignment to allow them to fit inside the body cavity. Snakes produce uric acid as a byproduct of protein synthesis, and expel it through the vent. This uric acid often looks like pieces of chalk, and is not soluble in water.

The nervous system of snakes is largely similar to that of other animals. The brain – which is relatively small and primitive – provides the control over the body by sending impulses through the spinal cord and nerves.

Reproductive Organs

Males have paired reproductive structures that they hold inside their tail base. The males evert these organs, termed hemipenes, during mating activities and insert them inside the females' cloacas.

Females have paired reproductive systems, which essentially mirror those of other vertebrates. One key difference is the presence of structures called oviducts. Oviducts hold the male's sperm and accept the eggs after they are released from the ovaries during ovulation.

The gender of snakes can be determined by passing a smooth, lubricated steel probe into the cloaca of a snake. When moved posteriorly, the probe will penetrate to a much greater depth in males than in females. This occurs because the inserted probe travels down the inside of one of the hidden hemipenes; when inserted into a female, no such space accepts the probe.

(Novices should not attempt to probe snakes. Most veterinarians, breeders and pet stores will perform the procedure for a nominal fee).

Shedding

Like other animals, snakes must periodically shed their outer skin layers. However, unlike mammals that do so continuously, snakes shed their entire external layer of skin cells periodically.

This process may occur as frequently as once every month when snakes are young and growing quickly, or as rarely as two or three times per year for larger, mature snakes.

Snakes that are injured, ill or parasitized may shed more frequently than usual. Some shedding events, such as the snake's first shed, or the females' pre-egg-laying shed, mark important milestones.

The shedding process takes approximately one week to complete. Initially, the snake begins producing a layer of fluid between the two outermost layers of skin. This serves as a lubricant that helps the old skin to peel off.

After a day or two, this fluid becomes visible in some species. It gives them a cloudy look, which, with experience, becomes very easy to spot. It is often most apparent when viewing the snake's ventral surface or eyes. Because a snake's eyes are topped with a clear scale, this fluid makes the eyes look very cloudy and blue. At this time, the snake's vision is seriously impaired, and most will spend their time hiding.

A few days later, the snake's eyes will clear up, and it will look normal again. A day or two later, the snake will begin the process of shedding.

The beginning of the shedding process starts with the snake trying to cut the old layer of skin on their lips. They do this by rubbing their face against some surface. While many keepers incorporate a rough surface in the cage for fear that the snake will not be able to facilitate his shedding process, in practice, this is rarely a problem. The cage walls are usually more than adequate.

After separating the skin on the lips, the old skin starts to peel away. The snake crawls forward, leaving the old skin behind. The new skin usually looks much brighter than normal.

Chapter 2: Kingsnake Color, Markings and Size

Part of the appeal of the genus *Lampropeltis* is the stunning array of colors and patterns represented by the various species and subspecies. In general, the patterns fall into one of several groups:

Black

Black kingsnakes (*Lampropeltis nigra*), Mexican black kingsnakes (*Lampropeltis nigritus*) and adult black milksnakes (*Lampropeltis gaigeae*) are mostly or completely black. Additionally, some Nuevo Leon kingsnakes (*Lampropeltis thayeri*) are nearly black.

In some cases, such as the black kingsnake, the black coloration likely serves a cryptic purpose. However, it is unclear what adaptive function – if any – the black color of the desert black kingsnake serves. In the case of black milksnakes, which often live at high altitudes, the color may serve as an adaptation for thermoregulation.

In some specimens of these species, faint pattern elements or scattered light-colored scales may be present. Many of these species display light colored pattern elements while they are young.

Tri-Colored

Herpetologists and herpetoculturists call snakes clad in red, white and black rings "tricolored." There is some degree of variation among tricolored snakes, as the red color may be better described as orange in some species, and the white bands may be yellow or peach-colored.

The width of the bands, number of bands and degree to which the bands encircle the belly vary from one species to the next, and, to some extent, between individuals.

One consistent feature of all tricolored Lampropeltis is that black bands separate the yellow and red bands.

Most North American milksnakes have tricolored color schemes, except the Eastern milksnake (*Lampropeltis triangulum triangulum*). The mountain kingsnakes (*Lampropeltis pyromelana* and *Lampropeltis zonata*) are tricolored as well, although their rings often break down on the sides.

Sinaloan milksnakes (*Lampropeltis triangulum sinaloae*) have broad red rings, while their yellow and black rings are narrow. By contrast, Pueblan Milksnakes (*Lampropeltis triangulum campbelli*) are clad in roughly equal sized bands of red, black and yellow or peach.

Bi-Colored

Some Central and South American milksnakes are essentially red snakes, with black rings or double-rings. Such feature red and orange bands, separated by black double-rings. Because these orange and red bands are very similar in color, it gives the snakes a bi-colored appearance.

Honduran milksnakes (*Lampropeltis triangulum hondourensis*) offer a good example of this color pattern, although some individuals have tricolored appearances, instead.

Blotched or Cross Barred

Eastern milksnakes (*Lampropeltis triangulum triangulum*), gray-banded kingsnakes (*Lampropeltis alterna*), some Nuevo Leon Kingsnakes (*Lampropeltis mexicana thayeri*), Mexican kingsnakes (*Lampropeltis mexicana*) and short-tailed kingsnakes (*Lampropeltis extenuata*) display blotched patterns.

The burrowing prairie kingsnakes and their relatives (Lampropeltis calligaster ssp.) are brown with reddish or darker brown blotches dorsally. The eastern (*Lampropeltis getula*) and California kingsnakes (*Lampropeltis californiae*) feature thin, light-colored bands on a dark ground color.

Speckled

The speckled (*Lampropeltis holbrooki*) and desert kings (*Lampropeltis splendida*) have dark ground colors, but many of the dark scales feature a light-colored center. Such snakes are often very attractive. The combination of dark ground colors and light colored speckles often gives the impression of a snake with an intermediate, solid color.

Some banded snakes feature scattered black scales on top of their light ground color. This is especially common among gray-banded kingsnakes (*Lampropeltis alterna*) and Honduran milksnakes (*Lampropeltis triangulum hondurensis*).

Striped

Generally, snakes that rely on crypsis and static defenses possess cross-barred patterns. By contrast, those that rely on locomotor defenses often have lengthwise stripes. However, there are some exceptions.

California kingsnakes (*Lampropeltis californiae*) feature a number of pattern variations that predominate in different geographic areas. One of these forms features a light, mid-dorsal stripe.

While it is not yet clear what, if any, adaptive advantage this pattern provides, hobbyists certainly appreciate these striped forms, which are popular in captivity.

Size

Kingsnakes vary greatly in size.

The smallest members of the genus *Lampropeltis* are the scarlet kingsnake (*Lampropeltis elapsoides*) and the short-tailed kingsnake (*Lampropeltis extenuata*). Both average about 14 to 20 inches in length, and are quite slender in build – particularly in the case of the short-tailed kingsnake. Both primarily subsist on elongate ectotherms, such as snakes and lizards.

The largest members of the genus Lampropeltis are the eastern kingsnakes (*Lampropeltis getula*) – particularly specimens from Florida (*Lampropeltis floridana*). Additionally, many of the Central and South American milk snakes reach large sizes as well. The Andean (*Lampropeltis triangulum andesiana*), black (*Lampropeltis triangulum gaigeae*) and Ecuadorian milksnakes (*Lampropeltis triangulum micropholis*) all attain 60-inches in length or more. Scattered reports allude to exceptionally large Eastern milksnakes (*Lampropeltis triangulum triangulum*) as well, although most specimens are less than 4 feet long.

While exceptionally large specimens are rarer than they used to be, the record for an eastern kingsnake (and likely, the genus as a whole) measured 82 inches (208 centimeters). (Florida Museum of Natural History, n.d.)

Chapter 3: Kingsnake Range and Habitat

1) Range

Kingsnakes are a wide-ranging collection of snakes, native to parts of North, Central and South America. If regarded as a single species, the milksnake (*Lampropeltis triangulum* ssp.) has one of the largest ranges of any snake in the world, being found from Ontario to Ecuador. However, the group likely represents several distinct species.

Some kingsnakes live in sympatry (share the same range) with each other, though few snakes that share the same resource base cohabitate. For example, eastern kingsnakes (*Lampropeltis getula*), mole kingsnakes (*Lampropeltis calligaster rhombomaculata*) and eastern milk snakes (*Lampropeltis triangulum triangulum*) may all inhabit the same acre in the Southeastern United States.

However, all three exploit difference niches. Eastern milk snakes prey primarily on lizards and small rodents, while mole kings prey on subterranean rodents and eastern kingsnakes prey on a virtually anything they can overpower, from snakes to birds to turtle eggs.

2) Habitat

The various kingsnake species utilize many different habitats. Some are comfortable within a wide range of habitat types, while others specialize in a very specific type of habitat.

One nearly universal characteristic among kingsnakes is their relatively secretive nature. In whichever habitat they dwell, the local species are likely to frequent secluded locations, such as rotted pine stumps, rodent burrows, rock crevices, among the roots of plants or under human-generated debris.

Generalists

Eastern kingsnakes, eastern milksnakes and California kingsnakes (*Lampropeltis californiae*) are examples of generalist species. These snakes may inhabit forests, riparian areas, agricultural lands and suburban areas. Many of the species that have expansive ranges are generalists; perhaps not coincidentally, these species often exhibit considerable local variation in terms of color and pattern.

Specialists

At the other end of the spectrum, some kingsnakes and milksnakes only thrive in a given habitat type. For example, gray-banded kingsnakes (*Lampropeltis alterna*) are restricted to a portion of the Chihuahuan Desert in southwest Texas and Northern Mexico. Likewise, scarlet kingsnakes (*Lampropeltis elapsoides*) are generally inhabits low-lying longleaf pine (*Pinus palustris*) forests of the American southeast.

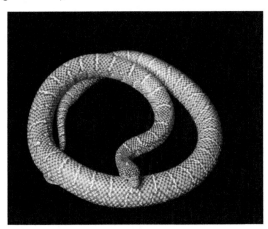

Chapter 4: Natural Behavior and Reproduction

1) Diel Cycle

Kingsnakes may be diurnal, nocturnal or crepuscular (active at dawn and dusk) depending on their species, habitat and the time of year.

Some species, such as gray-banded kingsnakes, are almost exclusively nocturnal, whereas Arizona mountain kingsnakes are primarily diurnal. Many milksnakes are nocturnal or crepuscular.

Individuals of some species vary their diel patterns – they may be diurnal during the spring and fall, while shifting to nocturnal patterns during the summer. Such a shift may allow the snakes to avoid the oppressive daytime temperatures, or take advantage of the warm nights.

Some species, such as Florida kingsnakes, exhibit an ontogenetic diel shift. Juveniles are nocturnal or crepuscular, but they become primarily diurnal as they approach 3-feet in length (KRYSKO1, 1995).

2) Seasonal Cycle

Snakes are ectothermic, or "cold-blooded," animals that rely on external energy sources to maintain their body temperature. This means that they are usually active when temperatures are near ideal levels.

Kingsnakes are most active in the spring. Mate searching, feeding and egg laying dominate the spring. Feeding is the name of the game during the summer, but if the temperatures become too hot, some may be forced to spend much of their time below ground or in other shelters.

In the fall, snakes continue to feed until the temperatures start dropping. At this time, they usually cease feeding and seek out suitable places to spend the winter. These can be deep rock crevices, rotten logs or rodent burrows.

Most kingsnakes enter a state of dormancy during the winter, called brumation. Brumation is essentially the reptilian equivalent of hibernation. Snakes sleep for most of this time, but they may emerge to bask or seek water on warm days.

Some species living in warm areas forgo a dormant period, entirely. Such species are more likely to reproduce at any time of the year, although mating activity usually remains concentrated in the spring.

3) Hunting Behavior

Most kingsnakes and milksnakes are active predators that prowl for prey. They use their forked tongue and vomeronasal system to locate lizards, snakes and rodents, whether that prey is active or sleeping.

Once located, the snake immediately grabs its prey with a quick, secure bite. Almost immediately, the snake throws several coils of its body around the animal, and then begins squeezing the prey – a technique known as constriction. After the prey has been incapacitated (usually from asphyxiation, although some may die from cardiac arrest), the snake begins to engulf it.

Usually, kingsnakes consume their prey headfirst. This helps the process of ingestion, as the fur, scales and limbs of the prey animal lay flat against the body when they are swallowed in this manner. If a snake swallows food backwards (which does occur from time to time), the prey's legs may splay outward, making the process more difficult.

Many kingsnakes and milksnakes utilize a significant length of their body when constricting prey, as opposed to boas, pythons and rat snakes, which only utilize a small portion of their length for constriction. This may relate to the differences in food, as kingsnakes frequently constrict elongate prey, such as snakes and lizards. By contrast, those snakes that only use a portion of their neck for constriction typically consume rodents or birds.

Kingsnakes may eat a number of prey items in quick succession, such as when they encounter a nest of rodents or a clutch of turtle eggs. However, they usually attack and consume prey items individually.

Once swallowed, kingsnakes retreat to a hiding spot to rest, bask to increase the rate of digestion, or they continue looking for other prey sources.

Prey is digested over the course of several days. Once completed, the snake passes a stool that contains most of the food residue from the meal. Hair, scales and other indigestible items are often seen in the feces.

4) Defensive Behavior

Kingsnakes are at risk to a variety of predators and they have evolved a number of effective anti-predator mechanisms to protect themselves.

The most important mechanism used by kingsnakes is crypsis – they use their colors and hiding abilities to avoid detection.

However, when a predator locates a kingsnake, the snake will engage in a variety of other behaviors to dissuade the predator.

Often, the first response of a discovered snake is to flee. Kingsnakes are not very fast, but if cover is nearby, they may be able to reach safety before the predator can grab them.

If escape is impossible, the kingsnake may become defensive. It will vibrate its tail rapidly in the leaf litter, which produces a sound that is reminiscent of that made by a rattlesnake. Whether this behavior is a specific attempt to mimic a rattlesnake or is just a generalized defense mechanism is unclear.

Kingsnakes may also flatten their heads or bodies when frightened. This causes the snakes to look larger, makes their pattern bolder and may cause the snake to resemble a venomous pit viper. The snake may even strike to enhance the charade.

If none of these defense mechanisms work, kingsnakes will emit an incredibly foul-smelling musk. Often, the snake will wave their tail back and forth while musking, which sprays the material all over the area. Often, kingsnakes also defecate and release urates when they discharge musk, causing the unpalatably potent concoction to become even viler.

If all of these methods fail, a kingsnake may attempt to bite the perceived adversary to defend itself. However, this is a largely ineffective method, as the small snakes are unlikely to bite hard enough to dissuade a hungry predator, such as a raccoon, hawk or skunk.

5) Batesian Mimicry

In addition to crypsis, musking, locomotor escape and biting, some kingsnake species employ a passive defense mechanism called Batesian mimicry.

Many kingsnakes are clad in red, yellow and black bands (often called "tri-colored"). Most authorities agree that these snakes bear such colors in order to resemble highly venomous coral snakes.

When predators locate such tri-colored serpents, it is thought, they avoid the kingsnakes, mistaking them for a dangerous species.

However, there are a few facts that are hard to reconcile with the notion that these snakes are demonstrating Batesian mimicry.

One of which is that tricolored *Lampropeltis* exist in many places that have no native coral snakes.

It is possible that the mimicry is directed at birds, who may have migrated from areas where coral snakes are native. Therefore, they may encounter coral snakes at other times.

It is also possible that coral snakes historically shared this range, but have since abandoned or become extirpated from these areas. Some evidence supports this hypothesis, as researchers have found coral snake fossils in Nebraska – far outside their current range.

Some scientists propose that the colors are actually cryptic, and do not serve as a mimicry at all. Those that advocate this position point to the nocturnal and secretive nature of the snakes as evidence of this. Additionally, many of the snakes' predators are nocturnal, and therefore, likely color-blind.

Another line of evidence that points to a cryptic function for the color pattern is the snakes' habit of stopping suddenly when they are fleeing a threat. In 2014, researchers at the University of North Carolina found that at least two tricolored *Lampropeltis* can crawl fast enough to create something called "flicker-fusion." This occurs when the rapid progression of color bands blurs the image of the snake to the predator's eyes, causing the snake to look one solid color. When the snake then stops, and the individual color bands "reappear," the snake appears to vanish from sight (Georgia C. TITCOMB, 2014).

In addition to tricolored mimicry, other kingsnakes may exhibit mimicry of pit vipers. For example, each of the varieties of the polymorphic gray-banded kingsnake may serve to mimic two different types of pit vipers.

For example, in the areas where banded rock rattlesnakes are found (*Crotalus lepidus klauberi*), alterna phase gray-banded kingsnakes – which look very similar to the rattlesnakes -- dominate. Conversely, in those areas inhabited by trans-Pecos copperheads, Blair's phase individuals are more common. The wide, red bands of Blair's phase snakes strongly resemble the bands of the copperheads – particularly at night. (Garstka, 1982)

Additionally, San Luis Potosi kingsnakes (*Lampropeltis mexicana*) strongly resemble Querataro Mountain rattlesnakes (*Crotalus triseriatus aquilis*). (Garstka, 1982)

Some researchers have argued that it would be difficult for mimicking species to evolve, as the intermediate forms would presumably provide poor camouflage, yet not provide the benefits of mimicry either. However, a 2009 study, published by the Royal Society, found evidence that this could happen, as long as the models (coral snakes) were sufficiently abundant (David W. Kikuchi, 2006).

The details of Batesian mimicry in Lampropeltis snakes promises to be a rich area of study for years to come.

6) Reproductive Cycle

Kingsnakes have an annual breeding cycle, but that does not mean that all mature adults successfully breed each year. This can occur because they cannot locate mates, could not access enough food to produce the necessary energy stores or because they became sick during this time of year.

While the specifics vary from one species to the next, males typically seek out females in the spring, shortly after emerging from brumation.

Once a suitable mate is found, the male crawls alongside the female, and wraps his tail around hers. He then everts one of his hemipenes and inserts it into her cloaca.

Mating can be a brief or extended affair. It normally lasts less than 30 minutes, but in some cases, it can last for hours. After mating is over, the male withdraws his hemipenis, and goes on his way.

Normally, mated pairs have no contact after breeding. The males do not participate in any part of the reproductive process after mating.

Eggs are deposited several weeks after mating in a secluded location, such as a rock crevice or hollow log. Approximately six to nine weeks later, the young kingsnakes will emerge from their eggs.

Left to their own devices, the young kingsnakes begin dispersing. They will undergo their first shed about one week after hatching, and soon thereafter, begin hunting small prey. Most kingsnake young resemble miniature versions of their parents, but a few species undergo color changes as they age.

Chapter 5: Ecology

The ecology of kingsnakes varies with the species and range, but most are small predators that primarily consume reptiles and small mammals. Birds of prey and medium-sized mammals are their primary predators. Larger snakes likely eat some of the smaller forms as well.

In some places – most notably the eastern United States – kingsnakes are among the largest snakes in the various regional habitats. For example, in the Pine Barrens of New Jersey, only the largest pine, rat and rattlesnakes grow larger than the local eastern kingsnakes. By contrast, small species of the central plains are some of the smallest species in the local snake community.

Kingsnakes are well-known ophidiophages, or snakes that eat other snakes. While most kingsnakes will eat other snakes when the opportunity arises, the tendency is more common in some forms than it is in others.

Most of the common kingsnakes (eastern, desert, black, speckled and California) are quite eager to pounce on a snake, while gray banded kingsnakes and eastern milksnakes are not as likely to do so (this does not mean they should be housed together!).

Most of the "getula complex" snakes are immune to the venom of native pit vipers, such as rattlesnakes, copperheads and cottonmouths. However, they are susceptible to the pit viper venoms of some foreign species.

It is unclear whether kingsnakes have any immunity to coral snake venom. This is of particular interest, as coral snakes are as eager to eat other snakes as kingsnakes are. Accordingly, their venom is very effective on most snakes. However, coral snakes only grow large enough to eat small kingsnakes.

Most pit viper venoms are more effective on rodents than reptiles, but there are exceptions. Cottonmouths – whose venom has no effect on eastern kingsnakes – use their venom to capture a wide range of prey, including fish, reptiles and amphibians.

These snake-eating habits often endear kingsnakes to the snake-fearing public. However, the public perception of these snakes is often flawed. Rather than deliberately seeking out rattlesnakes and killing them out of a sense of benevolence for the rest of the ecosystem, kingsnakes kill other snakes for food.

Like all other snakes, kingsnakes do not engage in unnecessary encounters with other animals. They only engage with other animals that they intend to eat or that represent an immediate threat.

Additionally, kingsnakes consume nonvenomous species in addition to native pit vipers. While venomous snakes may be abundant in an area, or they may share the same habitat, it is unlikely that kingsnakes prefer venomous snakes. Venom aside, a large pit viper can inflict two deep puncture wounds with their fangs, which may be very dangerous for a snake.

1) Predators

Typical predators of kingsnakes include:

Birds of prey, including hawks, eagles, falcons and owls

Herons and other wading birds

Raccoons (*Procyon lotor*)

Opossums (*Didelphis virginiana*)

Coatis (*Nasua* sp.)

Weasels, ferrets and their kin

Domestic dogs and cats

Other snakes, including kingsnakes and indigo snakes (*Drymarchon* sp.)

Additionally, individuals undoubtedly fall victim to crocodilians, large turtles, predatory fish, squirrels, jaguars, pigs, blue jays and other predators from time to time.

Young kingsnakes fall victim to far more predators than large kingsnakes do, and small forms fear more predators than larger forms.

Additionally, humans kill a large number of kingsnakes. This occurs directly, such as when people deliberately kill the animals or accidentally run them over (roads represent a high mortality threat for snakes), or indirectly, such as when humans destroy local habitats or pollute waterways, thus disrupting the local food chain.

2) Prey

In general, kingsnakes are opportunistic carnivores, but a few prey types feature predominately in their diets:

Lizards, especially skinks (*Plestiodon* sp.) and spiny/fence lizards (*Sceloporus* sp.)

Small mammals, for example, deer mice (*Peromyscus* sp.) and shrews (*Sorex* sp.)

Birds

Other snakes

(Fleet, 1970) (RODRIGUEZ-ROBLES, Feeding Ecology of the California Mountain Kingsnake, Lampropeltis zonata (Colubridae), 2003)

However, virtually any small creature may find itself starring down the business end of a hungry kingsnake. Kingsnakes occasionally eat things like reptile eggs (including those of lizards, snakes and turtles), frogs and salamanders as well.

Chapter 6: Etymology and Taxonomy

The word "Lampropeltis" literally means "shiny shield" or "radiant small shields." It is a reference to the group's shiny, smooth scales. This trait is common to all *Lampropeltis* species.

The term "getula" refers to the Getulian society of Morocco, who frequently used chain-link-like patterns in their art. The nominate form of the "getula-complex" is the eastern kingsnake, which features a chain-like color pattern.

"Triangulum," the species name for milksnakes, means "three angles," and is presumably a reference to the tri-colored pattern of most milksnakes.

Strangely, "calligaster," the species name of the prairie kingsnakes, means "beautiful stomach." It is unclear why this term was applied to these snakes.

Many of the sub specific terms associated with these snakes refer to their color pattern. For example, "alterna," the specific name for gray-banded kingsnakes, refers to the alternating bands on their backs. "Rhombomaculata," the sub specific name for the mole kingsnake, refers to the rhomboid-shaped spots along the snakes' backs. The terms "nigrita" and "nigritus" refer to the black coloration of black and Mexican black kingsnakes, respectively.

Other snakes have been named in honor of individuals. For example, "webbi," "nelsoni," "campbelli" and "conanti" are Latinized versions of people's names. "Californiae" refers to the common kingsnakes that are native to the state of California.

The taxonomy of the genus Lampropeltis is unsettled, and has been for some time. At high levels, most literature agrees with the treatment of the group, but the lower levels of taxonomy are in a constant state of flux.

All snakes are part of the Order Serpentes. Within this order, the kingsnakes are unambiguously placed within the Family Colubridae. However, the Family Colubridae is definitely polyphyletic, and taxonomists are likely to change the treatment of the group in the future.

Within the family, kingsnakes and their allies form the group Lampropeltini, which also includes several groups of other snakes, such as the gopher, bull and pine snakes (*Pituophis*) and the rat snakes (*Pantherophis, Bogertophis*), among others.

Within the group Lampropeltini, kingsnakes and milksnakes form the genus Lampropeltis. Because milksnakes are sometimes considered a single species, the milksnakes are essentially a type of kingsnake.

Beyond the level of genus, taxonomists and herpetologists have reached relatively little consensus. Nearly as quickly as studies and taxonomic treatments are published, contradictory studies emerge.

Accordingly, one authority may call a snake *Lampropeltis getula californiae*; another may consider the same snake *Lampropeltis californiae*.

For hobbyists, these changes are of little consequence (except in the rare cases where taxonomic treatment alters the legal status of a snake). Fundamentally, these changes are academic and should not cause unnecessary headaches.

Accordingly, it may be helpful for hobbyists to think about the different species and subspecies as belonging to different unofficial "forms" or "groups." Recognize the fact that snakes are labeled as a given species or subspecies, but know that in the future, many names are likely to change.

Getula Group

While many taxonomists recognize these individual forms as subspecies of a single species, others argue that each is a distinct subspecies. For example, the nominate form; the Eastern kingsnake, was initially considered *Lampropeltis getula getula*, while the California kingsnake was identified as *Lampropeltis getula californiae*. However, some authorities have elevated these different forms to the level of full species. (R. ALEXANDER PYRON1, 2009) In this framework, the snakes become *Lampropeltis getula* and *Lampropeltis californiae*.

The important thing to understand is that an eastern kingsnake is more closely related to a California kingsnake than it is to an eastern milksnake (*Lampropeltis triangulum triangulum*) or mole kingsnake (*Lampropeltis calligaster rhombomaculata*) – both of which live alongside it!

The getula group includes the eastern, black (*Lampropeltis nigra*), desert (*Lampropeltis splendida*), desert black (*Lampropeltis nigritus*), speckled (*Lampropeltis holbrooki*), California (*Lampropeltis californiae*) and – if recognized – the Florida kingsnake (*Lampropeltis floridana*). This includes all forms of Florida kingsnakes, including the Apalachicola lowland form, sometimes called *Lampropeltis getula goini* or *Lampropeltis getula meansi* (again, if recognized).

Calligaster Group

The *calligaster* group includes only three species. The mole kingsnake (*Lampropeltis calligaster rhombomaculata*), the prairie kingsnake (*Lampropeltis calligaster calligaster*) and the south Florida mole kingsnake (*Lampropeltis calligaster occioiptolineata*) all share broadly similar lifestyles. All three species are clad in brown. Prairie kingsnakes display bold color patterns, but both types of mole kingsnake may become nearly pattern less with age.

These medium to large kingsnakes all live subterranean lifestyles, consume rodents and are rarely encountered. Most authorities agree that these three snakes are each other's closest living relatives, and place them all in the same species. The three forms have a relatively contiguous distribution, covering the southeastern quarter of the United States.

Extenuata Group

The *extenuata* "group" consists of a single species – the short-tailed kingsnake (*Lampropeltis extenuata*). This species was only recently placed in the genus *Lampropeltis*, previously being called the short-tailed snake.

Short-tailed kingsnakes differ markedly from many other kingsnakes. They are exceptionally slender, very small and eat snakes exclusively. Short-tailed kingsnakes are semi-fossorial and rarely encountered.

Short-tailed kingsnakes are brown with darker blotches. They are an endemic and protected species in Florida. Accordingly, they are not available in the pet trade.

Some taxonomists consider the *Getula, Calligaster* and *Extenuata* groups to form a "super group" that is different from the other three groups.

Zonata / Pyromelana Group

The Arizona and California mountain kingsnakes (*Lampropeltis pyromelana* and *Lampropeltis zonata*, respectively) resemble milksnakes in most respects. Essentially similar to most other tricolored kingsnakes, their bands occasionally fail to reach all the way around their ventral sides.

Mountain kingsnakes primarily prey on lizards, but they eat rodents and birds when they are available. (RODRIGUEZ-ROBLES, Feeding Ecology of the California Mountain Kingsnake, Lampropeltis zonata (Colubridae), 2003)

Mountain kingsnakes are very attractive, and quite popular among hobbyists. Great emphasis is sometimes placed on the specific location from which a given snake's ancestors originated.

There is some dispute regarding the taxonomy within this group. Some authorities consider the Arizona mountain kingsnake to consist of two species: *Lampropeltis pyromelana* and *Lampropeltis knoblochi*; others consider them to be regional variants (subspecies) of the same species.

Triangulum Group

The *triangulum* group includes all of the milksnakes, although recent research suggests that the various species do not form a monophyletic group, which shares a single ancestor. In other words, while they are all kingsnakes, they form different lineages within the genus.

Most milksnakes are tri-colored or bi-colored, but the eastern milksnake (*Lampropeltis triangulum triangulum*) is blotched, and the black milksnake (*Lampropeltis gaigeae*) turns black as it matures.

Milksnakes are some of the most attractive kingsnakes, and they are quite popular among hobbyists. Most milksnakes prey on lizards in the wild, although some forms eat rodents and snakes as well.

In general, milksnakes are secretive and shy snakes, which are often nocturnal.

Mexicana / Alterna Group

The *Mexicana / alterna* group contains the gray-banded kingsnake (*Lampropeltis alterna*), Mexican kingsnake (*Lampropeltis mexicana*), Durango Mountain kingsnake (*Lampropeltis greeri*) The Queretaro Mountain kingsnake (*Lampropeltis ruthveni*) and Nuevo Leon kingsnake (*Lampropeltis thayeri*).

Some authorities also place Webb's kingsnake (*Lampropeltis webbi*) in this group as well. (Ruane, 2014)

These snakes tend to have large, distinct heads. Most are nocturnal species that hunt sleeping lizards. Many of these are polymorphic species, meaning that the offspring can have varied appearances.

In fact, the gray-banded kingsnake was considered two different species for a long time until researchers learned that the two snakes were simply different color forms of the same species. Some workers place the *triangulum* group within the *Mexicana/alterna* group. Others include the mountain kings in this group as well.

Example Taxonomies

The following are adapted from the taxonomies set forth by different authorities. Reasonable common names have been added to each for reference purposes.

Ruane et al. Taxonomy (2014)

Species	Common Name
calligaster	Prairie Kingsnake
zonata	California Mountain Kingsnake
webbi	Webb's Milksnake
pyromelana	Arizona Mountain Kingsnake
knoblochi	Chihuahuan Mountain Kingsnake
elapsoides	Scarlet Kingsnake
mexicana	Mexican Kingsnake
polyzona	Mexican Milksnake
ruthveni	Ruthven's Kingsnake
micropholis	South American Milksnake
abnorma	Central American Milksnake
extenuata	Short-tailed Kingsnake
nigra	Black Kingsnake
getula	Eastern Kingsnake

holbrooki	Speckled Kingsnake
splendida	Desert Kingsnake
californiae	California Kingsnake
alterna	Gray-Banded Kingsnake
annulata	Tamaulipas Milksnake
gentilis	Western Milksnake
triangulum	Eastern Milksnake

Integrated Taxonomic Information System (ITIS)

Species	Subspecies	Common Name
alterna		Gray-Banded Kingsnake
calligaster	*calligaster*	Prairie Kingsnake
calligaster	*occipitolineata*	South Florida Mole Kingsnake
calligaster	*rhombomaculata*	Mole Kingsnake
getula	*californiae*	California Kingsnake
getula	*floridana*	Florida Kingsnake
getula	*getula*	Eastern Kingsnake
getula	*holbrooki*	Speckled Kingsnake
getula	*nigra*	Black Kingsnake
getula	*nigrita*	Black Desert Kingsnake
getula	*splendida*	Desert Kingsnake
getula	*sticticeps*	Outer Banks Kingsnake
mexicana		Mexican Kingsnake
pyromelana	*infralabialis*	Utah Mountain Kingsnake
pyromelana	*pyromelana*	Arizona Mountain Kingsnake
pyromelana	*woodini*	Huachuca Mountain Kingsnake
ruthveni		Ruthven's Kingsnake
triangulum	*amaura*	Louisiana Milksnake
triangulum	*annulata*	Mexican Milksnake
triangulum	*celaenops*	New Mexico Milksnake
triangulum	*elapsoides*	Scarlet Kingsnake
triangulum	*gentilis*	Central Plains Milk Snake
triangulum	*multistriata*	Pale Milksnake
triangulum	*syspila*	Red Milksnake

triangulum	*taylori*	Utah Milksnake
triangulum	*triangulum*	Eastern Milksnake
zonata	*multicincta*	Sierra Mountain Kingsnake
zonata	*multifasciata*	Coast Mountain Kingsnake
zonata	*parvirubra*	San Bernadino Mountain Kingsnake
zonata	*pulchra*	San Diego Mountain Kingsnake
zonata	*zonata*	St. Helena Mountain Kingsnake

IUCN Redlist of Threatened Species

Species	Common Name
alterna	Gray-Banded Kingsnake
calligaster	Yellow-Bellied Kingsnake
catalinensis	Catalina Island Kingsnake
getula	Common Kingsnake
herrerae	Isla Todos Santos Milksnake
mexicana	Mexican Kingsnake
pyromelana	Sonoran Mountain Kingsnake
ruthveni	Ruthven's Kingsnake
webbi	Webb's Milksnake
zonata	California Mountain Kingsnake

The Reptile Database

Species	Subspecies	Common Name
alterna		Grey-banded Kingsnake
californiae		California Kingsnake
calligaster	*calligaster*	Prairie Kingsnake
calligaster	*occipitomaculata*	South Florida Mole Kingsnake
calligaster	*rhombomaculata*	Mole Kingsnake
elapsoides		Scarlet Kingsnake / Milksnake
extenuata		Short-Tailed Snake
getula		Eastern Common Kingsnake
holbrooki		Speckled Kingsnake
knoblochi		Chihuahuan Mountain Kingsnake

mexicana	*mexicana*	Mexican Kingsnake
mexicana	*thayeri*	Neuvo Leon Kingsnake
nigra		Black Kingsnake
pyromelana	*pyromelana*	Arizona Mountain Kingsnake
pyromelana	*infralabialis*	Utah Mountain Kingsnake
ruthveni		Ruthven's Kingsnake
splendida		Desert Kingsnake
triangulum	*triangulum*	Eastern Milksnake
triangulum	*abnorma*	Central American Milksnake
triangulum	*amaura*	Louisiana Milksnake
triangulum	*andesiana*	Andean Milksnake
triangulum	*annulata*	Mexican Milksnake
triangulum	*arcifera*	-
triangulum	*blanchardi*	Blanchard's Milksnake
triangulum	*campbelli*	Pueblan Milksnake
triangulum	*celaenops*	New Mexico Milksnake
triangulum	*conanti*	Conant's Milksnake
triangulum	*dixoni*	Dixon's Milksnake
triangulum	*gaigae*	Black Milksnake
triangulum	*gentilis*	Central Plains Milksnake
triangulum	*hondurensis*	Honduran Milksnake
triangulum	*micropholis*	-
triangulum	*multistrata*	Pale Milksnake
triangulum	*nelsoni*	Nelson's Milksnake
triangulum	*oligozona*	-
triangulum	*polyzona*	-
triangulum	*sinaloae*	Sinaloan Milksnake
triangulum	*smithi*	Smith's Milksnake
triangulum	*stuarti*	Stuart's Milksnake
triangulum	*syspila*	Red Milksnake
triangulum	*taylori*	Utah Milksnake
webbi		Webb's Kingsnake
zonata		California Mountain Kingsnake

40

SSAR 6th Edition (2008)

Species	Subspecies	Common Name
alterna		Gray-Banded Kingsnake
calligaster	*calligaster*	Prairie Kingsnake
calligaster	*occipitomaculata*	South Florida Mole Kingsnake
calligaster	*rhombomaculata*	Mole Kingsnake
extenuata		Short-Tailed Snake
getula	*getula*	Eastern Kingsnake
getula	*californiae*	California Kingsnake
getula	*floridana*	Florida Kingsnake
getula	*holbrooki*	Speckled Kingsnake
getula	*meansi*	Apalachicola Kingsnake
getula	*nigra*	Eastern Black Kingsnake
getula	*nigrita*	Western Black Kingsnake
getula	*splendida*	Desert Kingsnake
pyromelana	*pyromelana*	Arizona Mountain Kingsnake
pyromelana	*infralabialis*	Utah Mountain Kingsnake
triangulum	*amaura*	Louisiana Milksnake
triangulum	*annulata*	Mexican Milksnake
triangulum	*celaenops*	New Mexico Milksnake
triangulum	*elapsoides*	Scarlet Kingsnake
triangulum	*gentilis*	Central Plains Milksnake
triangulum	*multistriata*	Pale Milksnake
triangulum	*syspila*	Red Milksnake
triangulum	*taylori*	Utah Milksnake
triangulum	*triangulum*	Eastern Milksnake
zonata		California Mountain Kingsnake

Chapter 7: Kingsnakes as Pets

While kingsnakes make great pets, there are a number of things to consider before you acquire one of your own. Kingsnakes are living, breathing creatures that deserve the highest quality of life possible.

1) Understanding the Commitment

You will be responsible for your snake's well-being for the rest of its life. This is important to understand, as kingsnakes may live to be 20 years of age or more. Can you be sure that you will still want to care for your pet in 20 years?

It is not your snake's fault if your interests change. Neglecting your snake is wrong, and in some locations, a criminal offense. You must never neglect your pet, even once the novelty has worn off, and it is no longer fun to clean the cage.

Once you purchase a kingsnake, it is your responsibility until it passes away at the end of a long life, or you have found someone who will agree to take over the care of the animal for you. Understand that it may be very difficult to find someone who will adopt it for you.

Never release a pet snake into the wild.

Snakes introduced to places outside their native range can cause a variety of harmful effects on the ecosystem. Even if the snake is native to the region, it is possible that it has been infected with pathogens. If released into the wild, these pathogens may run rampant through the local population, causing horrific die offs.

2) The Costs of Captivity

Keeping a snake is much less expensive than many other pets; however, novices frequently fail to consider the total costs of purchasing the snake, its habitat, food and other supplies. In addition to the up-front costs, there are on-going costs as well.

Startup costs

One surprising fact for most new keepers is that the enclosure and equipment will often cost about twice what the animal does (this is not always the case with high-priced snakes). In some cases, the total habitat may cost three times the purchase price of the snake or more.

Prices fluctuate from one market to the next, but in general, the least you will spend on the snake is about $50 (£30), while the least you will spend on the habitat (and assorted equipment) will be $100 (£58).

Conversely, if you select an expensive snake and an elaborate habitat, you could easily spend more than $500 (£292).

Breeders and those with large collections often implement systems that reduce the per-snake housing costs, sometimes getting the costs down to one quarter of that price. However, for the hobbyist with a pet snake or two, such options are not helpful or appropriate.

Examine the charts on the following pages to get an idea of three different pricing scenarios. While the specific prices listed will vary based on numerous variables, the charts are instructive for first-time buyers.

The first details a keeper who is trying to spend as little as possible, while the second provides a middle-of-the-road example. The third example is of a more extravagant shopper, who wants an expensive snake, and top-notch equipment.

These charts do not cover all of the costs necessary at startup, such as the initial veterinary visit, shipping charges for the snake or any of the equipment (which can easily exceed $100) or the initial food purchase. These charts also fail to allocate anything decorative items, and they assume the use of newspaper as a substrate, which is essentially free.

Inexpensive Options

Eastern Kingsnake	$50 (£29)
Plastic Storage Box	$10 (£6)
Screen and Hardware for Lid	$10 (£6)
Heat Lamp Fixture and Bulbs	$20 (£11)
Digital Indoor-Outdoor Thermometer	$15 (£9)
Infrared Thermometer	$35 (£20)
Water Dish	$5 (£3)
Forceps, spray bottles, miscellaneous supplies	$20 (£11)
Total	**$165** (£96)

Moderate Option

Gray-Banded Kingsnake	$100 (£58)
10-Gallon Aquarium	$25 (£15)
Screen Lid	$10 (£6)
Heat Lamp Fixture and Bulbs	$20 (£11)
Digital Indoor-Outdoor Thermometer	$15 (£6)
Infrared Thermometer	$35 (£20)
Water Dish	$5 (£3)
Forceps, spray bottles, miscellaneous supplies	$20 (£11)
Total	**$230** (£134)

Premium Option

Albino Honduran Milksnake	$200 (£117)
Commercial Plastic Cage	$150 (£87)
Radiant Heat Panel	$75 (£44)
Thermostat	$50 (£29)
Digital Indoor-Outdoor Thermometer	$15 (£6)
Infrared Thermometer	$35 (£20)
Water Dish	$5 (£3)
Forceps, spray bottles, miscellaneous supplies	$20 (£11)
Total	**$550** (£322)

Ongoing Costs

Once you have your snake and his habitat, you must still be able to afford regular care and maintenance. While snakes are often described as very low-cost pets, this should be viewed in context.

Compared to a 100-pound Labrador retriever, a snake is relatively inexpensive. However, when compared to a goldfish, tarantula or hermit crab, snakes are fantastically expensive.

Here is an example of the ongoing costs a typical snake keeper must endure. Remember: Emergencies can and will happen. You must have some way to weather these storms, and afford a sudden $500 (£292) veterinary bill, or the cost to replace a cage when it breaks unexpectedly.

The three primary ongoing costs for snake are:

Veterinary Costs

While experienced keepers may be able to avoid going to the vet for regular observations, novices should visit their veterinarian at least once every six months. Depending on your vet's advice, you may only need to pay for an office visit. However, if your vet sees signs of illness, you may find yourself paying for cultures, medications or procedures. Wise keepers budget at least $200 to $300 (£117 to £175) for veterinary costs each year.

Food Costs

Virtually all kingsnakes will eat an average of one food item per week, but they may refuse the odd meal because they are shedding or simply do not want to eat. Accordingly, 50 items per year is a good estimate for the requirements of a kingsnake, regardless of the size or species. Some – such as mature males – will thrive on much less than this. Accordingly, your food costs depend almost entirely on two things: The size of the food item, and the route by which you acquire the food items.

For example, a hopper-sized or small adult mouse is sufficiently large to satiate even the largest scarlet kingsnakes (Lampropeltis elapsoides). Conversely, an exceptionally large eastern kingsnake (*Lampropeltis getula*) may be large enough to swallow small rats. This difference in prey size represents a five-fold difference in per-meal food costs.

The other primary factor influencing food costs is the source you use. Retail rodents are about three times the price of those purchased in bulk. However, to purchase bulk rodents, you must have a dedicated freezer in which to keep them. For those with one or two pet snakes, this is hardly cost effective.

Because of these factors, the cost to feed your kingsnake can vary by an order of magnitude. For example, a gray-banded kingsnake will likely eat pinkies or fuzzies for its first year of life. Newborn mice are often available for $0.25 (£0.15) or less. If you purchased these in bulk, your annual food bill (not including shipping – which will likely exceed the cost of the rodents) would be $12 (£7). By contrast, the owner of a large Florida kingsnake may be forced to buy 50 small rats a year. If purchased in a retail environment, the costs would exceed $150 (£87) each year.

Maintenance Costs

It is important to plan for routine and unexpected maintenance costs. Commonly used items, such as paper towels, disinfectant and aspen shavings are rather easy to calculate. However, it is not easy to know how many burned out light bulbs, cracked water dishes or faulty thermostats you will have to replace in a given year.

Keepers who keep small species in simple enclosures will likely find that $50 (£29) covers their yearly maintenance costs. By contrast, those keeping large animals in elaborate habitats are sure to spend $200 (£117) or more each year.

Always try to purchase frequently used supplies, such as light bulbs, paper towels and disinfectants in bulk to maximize your savings. It is often beneficial to consult with local reptile-keeping clubs, who often use their members combined needs to make purchases in bulk.

3) Myths and Misunderstandings

Snakes are the subject for countless myths and misunderstandings. It is important to rectify any flawed perceptions before welcoming a snake into your life.

Myth: Snakes grow in proportion to the size of their cage and then stop.

Fact: Snakes do no such thing. Healthy snakes grow throughout their lives, although the rate of growth slows with age. Placing them in a small cage in an attempt to stunt their growth is an unthinkably cruel practice, which is more likely to sicken or kill the snake than stunt its growth.

Myth: Snakes can sense fear.

Fact: Snakes are not magic creatures. They are constrained by physics and biology just as humans, dogs and squid are. That said, it is possible for some animals to read human body language as well as, or better than, other humans. Some long-time keepers have noticed differences in the behavior of some snakes when people of varying comfort levels handle them. This difference in behavior may be confused with the snake "sensing fear."

Myth: Snakes must eat live food.

Fact: While snakes primarily hunt live prey in the wild, some species consume carrion when the opportunity presents itself. In captivity, most snakes learn to accept dead prey. Whenever possible, hobbyists should feed their snakes dead prey to minimize the suffering of the prey animal and reduce the chances that the snake will become injured.

Myth: Snakes have no emotions and do not suffer.

Fact: While snakes have very primitive brains, and do not have emotions comparable to those of higher mammals, they can absolutely suffer. Always treat snakes with the same compassion you would offer a dog, cat or horse.

Myth: Snakes prefer elaborately decorated cages that resemble their natural habitat.

Fact: While snakes do thrive better in complex habitats that offer a variety of hiding and thermoregulatory options, they do not appreciate your aesthetic efforts.

Unlike humans, who experience the world through their eyes, snakes experience the world largely as they perceive it through their vomeronasal system. Your Honduran milksnake is not impressed with the rainforest wallpaper decorating the walls of his cage.

Additionally, while snakes require hiding spaces, they do not seem to mind whether this hiding space is in the form of a rock, a rotten log or a paper plate. As long as the hiding spot is safe and snug, they will utilize it.

4) Selecting Your Kingsnake

The various kingsnake species and subspecies come in so many different colors, patterns, sizes and personalities that it is difficult for a beginner to know where to start.

There are three primary considerations to make:

The Form (Species, Subspecies of Geographic Variant)

Research the various species of kingsnake to determine which one's characteristics appeal to you. The personality, feeding habits, natural history and size are all important aspects to consider, as is the range of the species.

Ideally, beginners would select an easy-to-care-for species, such as any of the *getula*-complex animals. *Calligaster*-complex animals are also easy to maintain, and they have a propensity for eating rodents.

Beginners should avoid difficult species, such as scarlet kingsnakes (*Lampropeltis elapsoides*), which are very small and difficult to entice to eat rodents. Small milksnake species are difficult to care for as well. By contrast, Honduran (*Lampropeltis triangulum hondurensis*), Sinaloan (*Lampropeltis triangulum sinaloae*) and Pueblan milksnakes (*Lampropeltis triangulum campbelli*) are generally easy to care for.

Beginners should give consideration for keeping snakes native to their region. Doing so makes climate control much easier.

The Gender

While the care of both genders is essentially identical (except for breeding maintenance), there are a few reasons for novice keepers to select males over females.

Even individually housed females may deposit eggs, which is hard on the female's body and carries some risk. Additionally, males are often available at lower prices than females are, because breeders desire for females, which inflates their price.

Nevertheless, there is no reason to avoid the purchase of a female, if she otherwise fits your criteria.

The Age

Whenever possible, new keepers should elect to purchase animals that are about 1 year old. Hatchlings are much more delicate than yearlings, which increases the chances of success.

Additionally, adult animals are often more intimidating to new keepers than smaller animals are. Choosing a less intimidating animal is helpful for many new keepers. There is also uncertainty regarding an adult's health and reproductive history, unless the snake comes from a very reliable source.

New keepers certainly can care for hatchlings or adults, but yearling animals are the best choice.

The Personality

Advanced hobbyists and breeders may consider a snake's personality to be a low priority in comparison to its species, gender, age and other factors. However, for the pet snake owner, personality is a very important factor.

While snakes are not individuals in the sense that humans or dogs are, they do vary in personality. Some are inherently docile, while a small percentage of any clutch may be downright hostile. Some are very shy, while others are more prone to prowling and exploring their cages. While these differences are often very subtle, they do exist, and it behooves the keeper to select a snake with a good personality.

Only rarely will you be able to select a snake from within a collection of his siblings, but if you are, look for the one that is the least shy. While this may leave you selecting one of the most aggressive or defensive hatchlings, most kingsnakes and milksnakes will outgrow this over time, and become trusting adults.

Ironically, these defensive snakes – which are the most likely to bite – are often the quickest ones to initiate feeding.

If you are purchasing a yearling or older animal, his personality is likely to remain relatively consistent from this point forward. Select a tame yearling, as most have already become excellent feeders.

5) Acquiring Your Kingsnake

If, after careful, deliberate, consideration you choose to purchase a kingsnake, you have a number of places, from which you can obtain one.

Pet Stores

Pet stores are a common place that many people turn to when they decide to purchase a snake. The benefits of shopping at a pet store are that they will likely have all of the equipment you may need, including cages, heating devices and food items. You will usually be able to inspect the snake up close and handle it before purchase. In some cases, you may be able to choose from more than one specimen. Further, many pet stores provide health guarantees for a short period. However, pet stores are retail establishments, and as such, you will pay more than you will from a breeder. Pet stores do not often know the pedigree of the animals they sell, nor are they likely to have date of birth, or other pertinent information on the snake.

Reptile Expos

Reptile expos are often excellent places to acquire new animals. Reptile expos often feature resellers, breeders and retailers in the same room, all selling various types of snakes and other reptiles. Often, the prices at such events are quite reasonable and you are often able to select from many different snakes. However, if you have a problem, it may be difficult to find the seller after the event is over.

Breeders

Breeders are the best place for most novices to shop. Breeders generally offer unparalleled information and support after the sale. Additionally, breeders often know the species well, and are better able to help you learn the husbandry techniques for the animal. The disadvantage of buying from a breeder is that you must often make such purchases from a distance, either by phone or via the Internet. Breeders often have the widest selection of snakes, and are often the only place to find rare species or color mutations.

Classified Advertisements

Newspaper and website classified advertisements sometimes include listings for kingsnakes. While individuals, rather than businesses generally post these, they are a viable option to monitor. Often these sales include a snake and all of the associated equipment, which is convenient for new keepers.

Chapter 8: Housing

Providing your kingsnake with appropriate housing is essential aspect of captive care. In essence, the habitat you provide to your snake becomes his "world."

In "the old days," those inclined to keep snakes had few choices with regard to caging. The two primary options were to build a custom cage from scratch or construct a lid to use with a fish aquarium.

By contrast, modern hobbyists have a variety of options from which to choose. In addition to building custom cages or adapting aquaria, dozens of different cage styles are available – each with different pros and cons.

Dimensions

Throughout their lives, snakes need a cage large enough to lay comfortably, access a range of temperatures and get enough room for exercise.

A good rule of thumb is to ensure that the snake is no longer than ½ of the cage's perimeter.

For example, a 55-gallon aquarium is about 48 inches long by 12 inches deep. This means that the perimeter of the aquarium is about 120 inches long, or 10 feet. Half of this is 60 inches / 5 feet, meaning that such an aquarium could comfortably house a 5-foot-long kingsnake. By way of another example, consider that a 10-gallon aquarium is about 20 inches long, by 11 inches wide. With a perimeter of 62 inches, the cage is suitable for a snake that is about 31 inches long.

Remember, this rule is a guideline for the *minimum* amount of space your snake requires. Always strive to offer the largest cage that you reasonably can. While many keepers suggest that large cages are intimidating to snakes, the truth is more subtle. Contrary to the popular notion, large cages –in and of themselves – do not cause snakes to experience stress.

Snakes live in habitats that exceed even the largest cages by several orders of magnitude. What snakes do not do, however, is spend much time exposed. Large, barren cages that do not feature complex cage props and numerous hiding places may very well stress snakes. However, large, complex habitats afford more space for exercising and exploring in addition to allowing for the establishment of a superb thermal gradient.

In addition to total space, the layout of the cage is also important – rectangular cages are strongly preferable for a variety of reasons:

They allow the keeper to establish more drastic heat gradients.

Cages with one long direction allow your snake to stretch out better than square cage do.

Front opening cages are easier to maintain when the cages are rectangular, as you do not have to reach as far back into the cage to reach the back wall.

Security

While kingsnakes are harmless animals, it is extremely important to consider cage security. Kingsnakes are escape artists – if it is possible to escape from the cage, they eventually will.

In most circumstances, if a snake can push its head through a crack, it can usually pull its entire body behind it.

Never use a cage to house kingsnakes if you are not certain that it is escape proof. Additionally, be sure to inspect all cages regularly to catch problems (such as a fraying bit of screen or a loose door gasket) before they are large enough to permit the snake to escape.

Aquariums

Aquariums are popular choices for snake cages, largely because of their ubiquity. Virtually any pet store that carries snakes also stocks aquariums.

Aquariums can make suitable snake cages, but they have a number of drawbacks. Aquariums are designed with fish in mind, not snakes; accordingly, most of the interior space is arranged in the vertical plane. While this is helpful for some species, kingsnakes do not climb very frequently. Most of this interior space will go unused.

Additionally, glass cages are hard to clean, and they are easy to break while you are carrying them around. Aquariums that are large are likely to be extremely heavy.

Aquariums are only enclosed on five sides, so keepers have to purchase or build a suitable lid for the enclosure. After-market screen tops are available, but often, they are not secure enough for kingsnakes.

Commercial Cages

Commercially produced cages have a number of benefits over other enclosures. Commercial cages usually feature doors on the front of the cage, allowing them to provide better access than top-opening cages do. Additionally, bypass glass doors or framed, hinged doors are generally more secure than after-market screened lids (as are used on aquariums) are.

Additionally, plastic cages are usually produced in dimensions that make more sense for snakes, and often have features that aid in heating and lighting the cage.

Commercial cages can be made out of wood, metal, glass or other substances, but the majority are PVC or ABS plastic.

Commercially cages are available in two primary varieties: those that are molded from one piece of plastic and those that are assembled from several different sheets. Assembled cages are less expensive and easier to construct, but molded cages have few (if any) seems or cracks in which bacteria and other pathogens can hide.

Some cage manufacturers produce cages in multiple colors. White is probably the best color for novices, as it is easy to see dirt, mites and other small problems. A single mite crawling on a white cage surface is very visible, even from a distance.

Black cages do not show dirt as well. This can be helpful for more experienced keepers who have developed proper hygiene techniques over time. Additionally, colorful kingsnakes often look very sharp against black cage walls.

While some snakes have cone cells in their retinas, and can presumably see color, it is unlikely that cage color is a significant factor in their quality of life. If you worry about the selection of color, it is probably best to choose a dark or earth-toned color.

Plastic Storage Containers

Plastic storage containers, such as those used for shoes, sweaters or food, make suitable cages for snakes if they are customized to make them secure. The lids for plastic storage boxes are almost never secure enough to be used for kingsnakes without the addition of supplemental security measures.

Hobbyists and breeders overcome this by incorporating Velcro straps, hardware latches or other strategies into plastic storage container cages. While these can be secure, you must be sure they are 100 percent escape-proof before placing a kingsnake in such cages.

The safest way to use plastic storage containers is with the use of a wooden or plastic rack. In such systems, often called "lidless" systems, the shelves of the rack form the top to the cage sitting below them. The gap between the top of the sides of the storage containers and the bottom of the shelves is usually very tight – approximately one-eighth inch or less.

When plastic containers are used, you must drill or melt numerous holes for air exchange. If you are using a lid, it is acceptable to place the holes in the lid; however, if you are using a lidless system, you will have to make the holes in the sides of the boxes.

All holes should be made from the inside towards the outside. This will help reduce the chances of leaving sharp edges inside the cage, which could cut the snake.

Homemade Cages

For keepers with access to tools and the desire and skill to use them, it is possible to construct homemade cages. However, this is not recommended for novice keepers, who do not yet have experience keeping snakes.

A number of materials are suitable for cage construction, and each has different pros and cons. Wood is commonly used, but must be adequately sealed to avoid rotting, warping or absorbing offensive odors.

Plastic sheeting is a very good material, but few have the necessary skills, knowledge and tools necessary for cage construction. Additionally, some plastics may have extended off-gassing times.

Glass can be used, whether glued to itself or with used with a frame. Custom-built glass cages can be better than aquariums, as you can design them in dimensions that are appropriate for snakes. Additionally, they can be constructed in such a way that the door is on the front of the cage, rather than the top.

Screen Cages

Screen cages make excellent habitats for some lizards and frogs, but they are poorly suited for most snakes. Screened cages do not retain heat well, and they are hard to keep suitably humid. Additionally, they are difficult to clean. Screen cages are prone to developing week spots that can give kingsnakes enough of a hole to push through and escape.

Chapter 9: Maintenance

1) Regular Tasks

Once you have decided on the proper cage for your situation and pet, you must keep your snake fed, hydrated and ensure that the habitat stays in proper working order. This will require you to examine the cage daily to ensure that your snake is healthy and happy.

Some tasks must be completed each day, while others are should be performed weekly, monthly or annually.

Daily

Monitor the ambient and surface temperatures of the habitat.

Ensure that the snake's water bowl is full of clean water.

Ensure that the snake has not defecated or produced urates in the cage. If he has, you must clean the cage.

Ensure that the lights, latches and other moving parts are in working order.

Verify that your snake is acting normally and appears healthy. You do not need to handle him to do so.

Ensure that the humidity and ventilation are at appropriate levels.

Weekly

Feed your snake (this may not be necessary each week).

Empty, wash and refill the water container.

Change the any sheet-like substrate.

Clean the walls of the enclosure.

Handle your snake (not after feeding time) and inspect him for any injuries, parasites or signs of illness.

Monthly

Break down the cage completely, remove and discard the substrate.

Clean the entire cage from top to bottom.

Sterilize the water dish and any other plastic or ceramic furniture in a mild bleach solution.

Measure and weigh your snake

Soak your snake for about 1 hour (Recommended, but not imperative).

Photograph your snake (Recommended, but not imperative).

Annually

Visit the veterinarian to ensure that your snake is in good health.

Replace the batteries in your thermometers and any other devices that use them.

2) Cleaning Procedures and Products

Cleaning a snake's cage or an item from his cage is relatively simple. Regardless of the way it became soiled or its constituent materials, the basic process is the same:

Rinse the object

Using a scrub brush or sponge and soapy water, remove any organic debris from the object.

Rinse the object thoroughly.

Disinfect the object.

Re-rinse the object.

Dry the object.

Scrub Brushes or Sponges

It helps to have a few different types of scrub brushes, sponges and similar tools. Use the least abrasive sponge or brush suitable for the task to prevent wearing out cage items prematurely. Do not use abrasive materials on glass or acrylic surfaces. Steel-bristled brushes work well for scrubbing wooden items, such as branches.

Soap

Use gentle, non-scented dish soap. Antibacterial soap is preferred, but not necessary. Most people use far more soap than is necessary -- a few drops mixed with a quantity of water is usually sufficient to help remove surface pollutants.

Bleach

Bleach (diluted to one-half cup per gallon of water) makes an excellent disinfectant. Be careful not to spill any on clothing, carpets or furniture, as it is likely to discolor the objects. Soak water bowls in this type of dilute bleach solution monthly. Always be sure to rinse objects thoroughly after using bleach and be sure that you cannot detect any residual odor.

Veterinarian Approved Disinfectant

Many commercial products are available that are designed to be safe for their pets. Consult with your veterinarian about the best product for your situation, its method of use and its proper dilution.

Steam Cleaners

Steam cleaners are very effective for sterilizing cages, water bowls and durable cage props after they have been cleaned. Steam is a very effective for sterilizing surfaces, and it will not leave behind a toxic residue. Never use a steam cleaner near your snake or any other living creatures.

Avoid Phenols

Always avoid cleaners that contain phenols, as they are extremely toxic to snakes. In general, do not use household cleaning products to avoid exposing your pet to toxic chemicals.

3) Keeping Records

It is important to keep records regarding your snake's health, feeding, shedding and other important details. In the past, snake keepers would do so on small index cards or in a notebook. In the modern world, technological solutions may be easier, such as using your computer or mobile device to keep track of the pertinent info about your snake.

While there is no limit to the amount of information you can record about your snake – and the more information to you record, the better – at a minimum, you should record the following.

Pedigree and Origin Information

Be sure to record the source of your pet, the date on which you acquired him and any other data that is available. If you purchase the snake from a quality breeder, you will likely be provided with information regarding the sire, dam, date of egg deposition, hatch date, weights and feeding records for the snake's entire life thus far.

Feeding Information

At a minimum, record the date and type of food item your snake eats at each feeding. If possible, record the time of day and weight of the food item as well. Additional notes may include techniques that were or were not successful, the color of the rodent or any scenting techniques used. It is also helpful to record refused meals as well.

Shedding Information

It is only necessary to record the date of each shed, but it may also be helpful to record the date you notice the snake's eyes turning blue. Additionally, be sure to note any shedding difficulties. If you have to take steps to rectify a bad shed, note these as well. It is helpful to note when snakes turn blue, as very rarely, snakes will clear up and fail to shed.

Weights and Length

At a minimum, you should record the weight of your snake monthly or each time he sheds. Because you look at your snake frequently, it is important to track his weight to ensure he is growing properly. If you like, you can measure his length as well, but doing so is very difficult to produce accurate results. There are computer programs that will calculate the length of your snake if you photograph him near a ruler.

Maintenance Information

Record the dates and details of any major maintenance. For example, while it is not necessary to note that you topped off the water dish each day, it is appropriate to record the dates on which you change the substrate, or sterilize the cage.

Breeding Information

If you intend on breeding your snake, you should record all details regarding the pre-breeding conditioning, cycling, introductions, copulations, ovulation, pre-lay shed and egg deposition.

Record all pertinent information about the egg clutch as well, including incubation technique, temperature and duration.

Record Keeping Samples

The following are two different examples of suitable recording systems. The first example is reminiscent of the style of card that many breeders and experienced hobbyists use. Because such keepers often have numerous snakes, the notes are very simple, and require a minimum amount of writing or typing.

Note that in this example, the keeper has employed a simple code, so that he or she does not have to write out "fed this snake one small, thawed mouse."

ID Number:	44522	Genus: Species:	Lampropeltis californiae	Gender: DOB:	Male 6/13/12	CARD #6
5.30.13 MM	6.07.13 MM	6.20.13 REFUSED LM	7.01.13 2MM	7.08.13 MM		
6.03.13 SHED /255g	6.11.13 MM	6.22.13 REFUSED MM	7.04.13 REFUSED LM	7.13.13 MM		
6.04.13 2SM	6.14.13 MM	6.30.13 SHED / 275g	7.05.13 MM			
SM= Small Mouse	MM= Medium Mouse	LM = Large Mouse				

The second example demonstrates a simple approach – keeping notes on paper – that is employed by many novice keepers. Such notes could be taken in a notebook or journal, or simply typed into a word processor. It does not ultimately matter how you keep records, just that you do keep records.

Date	Notes
6-20-13	*Acquired "King Solomon" the kingsnake from Joe Q. Snake breeder. Joe explained that Solomon is a striped California kingsnake (Lampropeltis californiae). Cost was $50 at the reptile expo down by the beach. Joe was not sure what sex Solomon was. Joe said he hatched last June, but he does not know the exact date. Solomon is about 16-inches long.*
6-21-13	*Solomon spent the night in the container I bought him in, I purchased a 20-gallon aquarium, screened lid and heat lamp at the pet store. Bought the thermometer at the hardware store next door and ordered a non-contact thermometer online. I am using old food containers for his water dish and hide boxes.*
6-24-13	*Solomon shed today! He looks beautiful. Everything came off in one long piece.*
6-25-13	*Fed Solomon a small thawed mouse today. I think I need longer tweezers! He was hungry!*
6-29-13	*Since Solomon looked so hungry, I fed him another thawed mouse today.*
7-5-13	*Fed Solomon one mouse. This one was brown, instead of white, but he didn't care.*

If you use small index cards or similar records, your pet will accumulate many cards over time. Paper clip the cards together so that you have easy access to the snake's history.

If you ever sell your snake or give him to a friend, make sure to pass along your records to the snake's new owner. Additionally, be sure to bring the records with you whenever you visit the veterinarian's office.

Chapter 10: Feeding

Kingsnakes are obligate carnivores that consume a wide variety of prey in the wild. Generalizations about the diet of the group are difficult to make, as so many different forms exist. For example, a mole kingsnake (*Lampropeltis calligaster rhombomaculata*) may eat rodents its whole life, while a gray-banded kingsnake (*Lampropeltis alterna*) may live almost exclusively on lizards.

Variety also exists among some species and subspecies: Eastern kingsnakes (*Lampropeltis getula*) may consume a frog, water snake, lizard and rodent in consecutive meals.

Short-tailed kingsnakes (*Lampropeltis extenuata*) feed almost exclusively on small snakes. It is unclear if they will accept alternative prey in captivity, but currently, this is not important for hobbyists, as they are a protected species.

1) Live, Fresh Killed or Frozen

Whenever possible, snakes should be fed dead prey. Most often, this comes in the form of frozen-thawed rodents.

While kingsnakes are perfectly capable of killing and consuming small rodents, birds or lizards, these animals often fight back. If the snake does not grab its prey correctly, the creature may be free enough to bite or scratch the snake. Such bites can cause serious injuries to snakes, especially if they occur on the snake's head. Additionally, it is far more humane for prey animal to be humanely euthanized than it is to be bitten, constricted and eaten by a snake.

Whenever thawing rodents, do so in warm water or at room temperature. Never attempt to thaw a rodent in the microwave.

2) Prey Species

In most circumstances, kingsnakes should be fed commercially raised rodents. However, if you have a supply of captive produced lizards, most species will likely thrive. However, it is important to avoid feeding snakes wild-caught lizards, which are likely to have parasites.

Some hobbyists offer their snakes a wider variety of food sources. While this may provide some small health benefits, many generations of snakes have been successfully raised solely on a diet of lab-raised rodents. Chicks are one potential alternative, although bird-eating snakes often produce soft, offensive smelling feces. Additionally, the chance of transmitting salmonella to your snakes by feeding them raw chicks is higher than it is with most other food sources.

Frogs or lizards can be offered to your kingsnake, but they must be captive raised and free of parasites or pathogens. You must choose a frog species that does not produce toxic secretions, such as American toads (*Bufo americanus*) or Pickerel frogs (*Rana palustris*). As alternative food items are unlikely to be economically viable over the long term, they are usually avoided in favor of rodents.

Young rabbits are an acceptable food source for kingsnakes that are large enough to eat them. Rabbits look a little larger than they actually are, as they normally adopt a "curled up" posture. Once relaxed, rabbits are very similar to rats in overall proportion. Rabbits are widely available as frozen-thawed feeders, but it can be challenging to find small enough rabbits to be applicable for kingsnakes.

3) Prey Size

While some snakes can consume very large food sources, kingsnakes are not boa constrictors that can swallow a monkey and digest it slowly over a month's time. Kingsnakes often consume prey that represents a significant portion of their body weight, but they do not eat prey of considerable girth. For example, kingsnakes may consume a snake that is nearly their length, but they do not consume large, bulky prey very often.

This means that captive snakes are best fed small prey items, on a more frequent schedule. In general, feed your kingsnake prey that is about the same thickness as the snake at mid-body or slightly larger.

4) How to Offer Food

Always offer food to your snake when the room is calm and free of pets, rowdy children, and other distractions. Frightened or stressed snakes rarely eat.

Some snakes prefer to eat in low light conditions, while others may respond best during the middle of the day. Use your species' natural history habits to make a good first guess, and adjust as necessary.

The first step in feeding is to gather thawed, dry rodent and a pair of long forceps, tweezers or tongs. Then, open the cage door or remove the lid and set it aside.

Grab the food item with the forceps. Grip it behind the shoulder blades so that you can produce realistic movements with the item.

Move the food item about 3 or 4 inches in front of the snake's nose. If he is hungry and ready to eat, he may begin flicking his tongue. If so, you can gently place it closer to his face, wiggling it slightly.

Be patient, and allow the snake to gather his nerve and strike the food item. As soon as the snake strikes, try to release the mouse. With a bit of luck, the snake will constrict the rodent as if it were alive. Once this happens, slowly move back and out of the snake's line of sight.

Check on the snake in about five minutes, and be sure that he is still eating the rodent. (Do not leave the area where your snake is with the cage door open. If you can observe it from a distance, leave the door or lid open while backing away. If this will not be possible, try to close the cage as slowly as possible to prevent spooking the snake).

Some snakes are prone to "forgetting" their dinner after they constrict it for a moment. This is usually not a big problem, as most snakes will accept the same rodent if re-offered. Some keepers have found that if you twitch the rodent slightly once the kingsnake has constricted it (to simulate the struggles of the rodent) it may help keep the snake focused on the job.

If your snake does not begin tongue flicking when presented with the rodent, try to animate the rodent's movements a little. Wiggle it from left to right quickly and try to elicit tongue flicks.

Investigatory tongue flicks are different from causal, exploratory flicks. They are much more rapid, deliberate and the tongue often remains extended for a prolonged period of time.

If your movements do not generate any interest in the snake, gently move the rodent until it contacts the snake's nose gently. If successful, this may finally get the snake's attention, but often it will cause the snake to flee. If this happens, discard the rodent, replace the cage lid and try again in a day or two.

Do not despair if your snake does not eat the first time you offer food. Many times, the snake may still be adjusting to his new home. Alternatively, he could be entering a shed cycle, during which time most snakes refuse food.

If your snake fails to eat after three different attempts, wait one full week before trying again. This should be enough time to allow him to shed or make it obvious that he is about to do so (opaque eyes, milky look to the skin).

5) Problem Feeders

It is not always possible to get a baby snake to begin accepting food voluntarily – this is when purchasing a snake from a reputable breeder pays off. Few breeders will sell their snakes before they are accepting food regularly and eagerly. If repeated attempts fail to yield positive results, you must take steps to jumpstart the process.

Once the snake refuses food for the fourth time (with at least one week elapsing to ensure shedding cycles are not the problem) contact the breeder, if you have not done so already.

Often, the breeder will be able to offer you tips or suggestions that may bring success. If you purchased the snake from a retail establishment, you can request suggestions, but substantial help is not as likely to follow.

Hidden Food

Some kingsnakes – particularly gray-banded kingsnakes—seem to eat more readily if they are allowed to find their food as they would in the wild. To do so, place a thawed pinky under a hide in the snake's cage right before the lights go off for the night.

Check on your snake in the morning – with luck, he will have found and devoured the pinky during the night.

Never do this with a live rodent. Pinkies would quickly become chilled, suffer and likely die. Furred rodents on the other hand may bite your snake and cause it serious injury.

Small Container

Sometimes, you can convince a small kingsnake to eat by simply placing it in a small container with a food item. Leave the snake alone like this overnight, and it may decide to eat. Never do this with a live rodent, as it may injure or kill your snake.

Dirty Mouse

Some snakes seem to be more likely to eat rodents that smell "dirty." To do so, place your rodent in a small container with some grass clippings and a bit of clean soil. Shake the container around gently, and offer the rodent as per usual.

Scent Transfer

Scent transfer seeks to make a young rodent smell like a natural food item for a young kingsnake, which is usually a lizard. Scent transfer is preferable to offering lizards outright, as it is less likely to cause parasite transmission.

To do so, wash a pinky mouse with soap and water. Rinse it thoroughly and pat dry with a paper towel. It is now ready to be coated in lizard scent.

There are a variety of ways to get a lizard's scent on the rodent. Most are effective, but take care should to avoid stressing the lizard unnecessarily.

You can gently rub the pinky on the lizard's head, tail and vent. Alternatively, you could place the rodent in the lizard's cage for a length of time. If the lizard has recently shed, small pieces of shed skin can be attached to the pinky.

Once you feel that the rodent smells like a lizard, offer it as per usual.

The most effective lizards for scent transfer techniques for kingsnakes are fence lizards (*Sceloporus* sp.), anoles (*Anolis* sp.) and skinks (*Plestiodon* sp.). However, many different species may work, including species that kingsnakes would never encounter – such as leopard geckos (*Eublepharis macularius*).

While lizards are the most effective species to use for scent transfer techniques with kingsnakes, snakes, frogs, chicks and other animals may be useful for some specimens.

If your kingsnake seems to appreciate the scent of birds, consider using chicken stock to scent the rodent (never cross-contaminate human food with reptile husbandry procedures).

Brained

WARNING: NOT FOR THE SQUEAMISH

For reasons that remain mysterious, some snakes seem more interested in frozen-thawed rodents when the skull is split open and the brains are smeared on the rodent's head. This is not easy to accomplish with rodents that are furred, as their skulls are more rigid.

To do so, a stainless steel probe or another clean instrument can be pressed into the rodent's skull. When it pierces the skull, use some of the brains to coat the skull.

Offer the rodent as you normally would.

6) Feeding Frequency

Most kingsnakes will thrive on a diet of one suitably sized rodent per week. For adults, this may even be excessive and cause them to gain weight.

Most snakes consume between two and four times their body mass per year (Rossi, 2006). Therefore, if you intend to feed your 1-pound snake once per week, each meal should be roughly 0.05 to .1 pounds, which is approximately the weight of a large adult mouse.

If faster growth is desired, young kingsnakes can be fed more often than this. With proper husbandry, kingsnakes can consume a prey item every two or three days. This will result in very rapid growth, and may cause snakes to mature in as little as 18 months.

Once the snake has reached the size where furred rodents are appropriate, they will not digest their prey as quickly, and feeding should be slowed.

7) Avoiding Regurgitation

If a snake is stressed or exposed to inappropriate temperatures, it may vomit any recently eaten food items. In addition to being a very unpleasant mess to clean up and a waste of money, vomiting is hard on the snake's body.

To avoid vomiting, always ensure your snake's habitat is the proper temperature, especially after eating. Additionally, refrain from handling your snake as long as a visible lump is present in his body. Even if the food item is too small to make a noticeable lump, refrain from handling a snake for at least 24 hours after feeding them.

If your snake vomits a food item, clean the cage immediately. Additionally, ensure that your snake can rehydrate properly. Many experienced keepers make it a practice to soak snakes after vomiting to ensure hydration.

Give snakes that vomit at least one full week before offering food again.

Chapter 11: Water and Humidity

Like most other animals, kingsnakes require regular access to clean drinking water to remain healthy. However, the amount of water in the air (humidity) is an important factor in their health as well.

Drinking Water

Kingsnakes require regular access to clean, fresh water. Provide this by means of a small to medium-sized bowl or dish. While it is acceptable to offer the snakes a bowl that will accommodate the snake, be sure to avoid filling such containers too high, as they are apt to overflow if the snake crawls into the bowl.

However, this is not necessary, and many keepers use bowls with 2- to 4-inch diameters. In fact, for species from arid habitats, it is better to err on the side of caution and avoid using a large water dish.

Kingsnakes are active creatures that are apt to tip their water bowl, so use a bowl heavy or wide enough that the snake will not tip it inadvertently.

Be sure to check the water dish daily and ensure that the water is clean. Empty, wash and refill the water dish any time it is contaminated with substrate, shed skin, urates or feces.

Some keepers prefer to use dechlorinated or bottled water for their kingsnakes, however untreated tap water is used by many keepers with no ill effects.

Soaking Water

In addition to providing drinking water, many keepers soak their snakes periodically in a tub of clean, lukewarm water. Soaking is helpful tool for the husbandry of many snakes, including kingsnakes. In addition to ensuring that your snake remains adequately hydrated, soaks help to remove dirt and encourage complete, problem-free sheds. It is not necessary to soak your snake if it remains adequately hydrated, but most kingsnakes benefit from an occasional soak.

Soaks should last a maximum of about one hour, and be performed no more often than once per week (unless the snake is experiencing shedding difficulties).

When soaking your snake, the water should not be very deep. Never make your snake swim to keep its head above water. Ideally, snakes should be soaked in containers with only enough water to cover their back. This should allow your snake to rest comfortably with its head above water.

Never leave a snake unattended while it is soaking.

Cage Humidity

In general, kingsnakes require moderate humidity levels. Kingsnakes from arid habitats, such as desert, desert black and gray-banded kingsnakes should have humidity between about 30 and 50 percent. By contrast, kingsnakes from humid habitats, such as eastern kingsnakes and Louisiana milk snakes, can tolerate humidity levels of 60 percent or higher, as long as they have ideal temperatures and the habitat remains clean.

Chapter 12: Cage, Furniture and Decorations

Strictly speaking, it is possible to keep a kingsnake in a cage devoid of anything but a substrate that permits burrowing and a water bowl. However, it is very beneficial to provide complex environments, with numerous hiding opportunities in the cage.

Additionally, many keepers enjoy decorating the cage to resemble the animal's natural habitat. While such measures are not necessary from the snake's point of view, if implemented with care, there is no reason not to decorate your pet's cage, if you are inclined to do so. However, it is recommended that beginners use a simple cage design for their first 6 to 12 months while they learn to provide effective husbandry.

Kingsnakes are secretive creatures. In the wild, they use rodent burrows, tree stumps, rock crevices, rotten logs and debris as hiding spots. (David A. Steen1, 2010) If they do not have a reason to expose themselves to predators, they do not. While this is sometimes disappointing to beginning snake keepers, it is necessary to allow your snake to spend much of its time hiding so that it feels secure and stress-free.

Snakes will move about to find water, food, mates or appropriate environmental conditions. Each species (and individual) has a different typical activity level – some of the racers (*Coluber* sp.) and whip snakes (*Masticophis* sp.) may be accustomed to traveling many miles each day in search of food, but kingsnakes travel relatively little.

Accordingly, it is imperative to provide your kingsnake with hiding opportunities.

1) Hide Boxes

"Hide boxes" come in a wide variety of shapes, sizes and styles. Some keepers use modified plastic or cardboard containers, while others use realistic looking logs and wood pieces. Both approaches are acceptable, but all hides must offer a few key things:

Hides should be safe for the snakes, and feature no sharp edges or toxic chemicals.

Hides should accommodate the snake, but not much else. They should be only slightly larger than the snake's body when it is laying in a flat coil.

Hides should have low profiles. Snakes prefer to feel the top of the hide contacting the dorsal surface of their body.

Hides either must be easy and economical to replace or constructed from materials that are easy to clean.

Plastic Storage Boxes

Just as a plastic storage box can be converted into an acceptable enclosure, small storage boxes can be converted into functional hiding places. Food containers, shoeboxes and butter tubs can serve as the base. If the container has a low profile, it needs only have a door cut into the tub. Alternatively, you can discard the lid, flip the tub upside down and cut an entrance hole in the side.

Plant Saucers

The saucers designed to collect the water that overfills potted plants make excellent hiding locations. All you have to do is flip them upside down and cut a small opening in the side for a door. Clay or plastic saucers can be used, but clay saucers are hard to cut. If you punch an entrance hole into a clay saucer, you must sand or grind down the edges to prevent hurting your snake.

Plates

Plastic, paper or ceramic plates make good hiding locations in cages that use particulate substrates. This will allow the snake to burrow up under the plate through the substrate, and hide in a very tight space. Such hiding places also make it very easy to access your snake while he is hiding.

Cardboard Boxes

While you must discard and replace them anytime they become soiled, small cardboard boxes can make suitable hide boxes.

Commercial "Half-Logs"

Many pet stores sell U-shaped pieces of wood that resemble half of a hollow log. While these are sometimes attractive looking items, they are not appropriate hide spots when used as intended. The U-shaped construction means that the snake will not feel the top of the hide when he is laying inside. These hides can be functional if they are partially buried, thus reducing the height of the hide.

Cork Bark

Real bark cut from the Cork Oak (*Quercus suber*), "cork bark" is a wonderful looking decorative item that can be implemented in a variety of ways. Usually cork bark is available in tube shape or in flat sheets. Flat pieces are better for most kingsnakes, although exceptionally large snakes may be able to use tubular sections adequately. Flat pieces should only be used with particulate, rather than sheet-like substrates so that the snake can get under them easily.

Scarlet kingsnakes (*Lampropeltis elapsoides*) and other species that frequently inhabit the space between the bark and the wood of standing, dead trees may utilize vertically placed slabs of cork bark as well.

Cork bark may be slightly difficult to clean, as its surface contains numerous indentations and crevices. Use hot water, soap and a sturdy brush to clean the pieces.

Commercially Produced Plastic Hides

Many different manufacturers market simple, plastic, hiding boxes. These are very functional if sized correctly, although some brands tend to be too tall. The simple design and plastic construction makes them very easy to clean.

Paper Towel Tubes

Small sections of paper towel tubes make suitable hiding spots for small kingsnakes and milksnakes. They do not last very long, so they require frequent replacement. They often work best if flattened slightly.

Newspaper or Paper Towels

Several sheets of newspaper or paper towels placed on top of the substrate (whether sheet-like or particulate) make suitable hiding spots. Many professional breeders use paper-hiding spaces because it is such a simple and economically feasible solution. Some keepers crumple a few of the sheets to give the stack of paper more height.

Unusual Items

Some keepers like to express their individuality by using unique or unusual items as hiding spots. Some have used handmade ceramic items, while others have used skulls or turtle shells. If the four primary criteria previously discussed are met, there is no reason such items will not make suitable hiding spaces.

2) Humid Hides

In addition to security, snakes also derive another benefit from many of their hiding spaces in the wild. Most hiding places feature higher humidity than the surrounding air.

By spending a lot of time in such places, snakes are able to avoid dehydration in habitats where water is scarce. Additionally, sleeping in these humid retreats aids in the shedding process. You should take steps to provide similar opportunities in captivity. Humid hides can be made by placing damp sphagnum moss in a plastic container. The moss should not be saturated, but merely damp. You can also use damp paper towels or newspaper to increase the humidity of a hide box. Some keepers prefer to keep humid hides in the habitat at all times, while others use them periodically – usually preceding shed cycles. Humid hides should never be the only hides available to the snake. Always use them in addition to dry hides.

3) A Final Word about the Importance of Hides

With relatively few exceptions, snakes will become severely stressed if they are forced to remain in the open at all times. In addition to health problems that may result, it is likely to affect your pet's personality as well. Snakes that are constantly stressed are more likely to exhibit defensive behaviors when they are handled.

In the wild, hiding spaces are rarely difficult for snakes to find. Provide them with the same opportunity in captivity. Because snakes are likely to select security over all other criteria, it is best to place hides at different parts of the thermal gradient. Additionally, it is wise to include humid and dry hides to the greatest extent possible.

Chapter 13: Substrates

Substrates are used to give your snake a comfortable surface on which to crawl and to absorb any liquids present. There are a variety of acceptable choices, all of which have benefits and drawbacks. The only common substrate that is never acceptable is cedar shavings, which emits fumes that are toxic to snakes.

Paper Products

The easiest and safest substrates for kingsnakes are paper products in sheet form. While regular newspaper is the most common choice, some keepers prefer paper towels, unprinted newspaper, butcher's paper or a commercial version of these products.

Paper substrates are very easy to maintain, but they do not last very long and must be completely replaced when they are soiled. Accordingly, they must be changed regularly -- at least once per week.

Use several layers of paper products to provide sufficient absorbency and a little bit of cushion for the snake.

Aspen

Shredded aspen bark is a popular substrate choice that works very well. Aspen shares most of the concerns that other particulate substrates do (ingestion hazards, increased labor), but it is likely the best of the particulate substrates for kingsnakes.

Aspen can be dusty, so look for brands that are advertised as "low dust." Aspen does not resist decay well, and you must keep it rather dry. This is fine for most kingsnakes, who prefer moderate humidity levels.

Aspen can be spot cleaned daily, but like most other particulate substrates, you must replace it completely every month.

Pine

Some hobbyists eschew pine, which is sometimes thought to produce irritating fumes. While this may be true of products made from the xylem (wood) of pine trees, it is not true of products made from the bark. Eastern kingsnakes (*Lampropeltis getula*) and scarlet kingsnakes (*Lampropeltis elapsoides*) are certainly common in pine forests, they often inhabit pine stumps and they experience no ill effects when kept on pine bark substrates.

Pine bark is not very absorbent, but it resists decay reasonably well. Pine bark is attractive and natural looking, but it does leave copious amounts of black dust inside the cage.

It can be spot cleaned daily, but requires monthly replacement.

Orchid Bark

The bark of fir trees is often used for orchid propagation, and so it is often called "orchid bark." Orchid bark is very attractive, though not quite as natural looking as pine bark. However, it exceeds pine in most other ways except cost.

Orchid bark absorbs water very well, so keepers who maintain rainforest species often use it, but it is useful for forest-dwelling snakes, like eastern kingsnakes (*Lampropeltis getula*), as well.

Because orchid bark is often reddish in color, it is very easy to spot clean. However, monthly replacement can be expensive for those living in the eastern United States and Europe.

Cypress Mulch

Cypress mulch is a popular substrate choice for many tropical species, but it is often too damp for use with kingsnakes from arid climates.

One significant drawback to cypress mulch is that some brands (or individual bags among otherwise good brands) produce a stick-like mulch, rather than mulch composed of thicker pieces.

These sharp sticks can injure the keeper and the kept. It usually only takes one cypress mulch splinter jammed under a keeper's fingernail to cause them to switch substrates.

Pulp Products

Many commercial pulp products have become available over the last decade. Comprised of recycled wood fibers, these products are very absorbent, but pose an ingestion hazard as they may swell once inside a snake's digestive system.

These products often absorb odors and liquids well, but with proper cage hygiene, snake cages should not emit objectionable odors.

Substrate Comparison Chart

Substrate	Pros	Cons
Newspaper	Safe, free, easiest substrate for keeping the cage clean.	May be unattractive to some. Purchase pre-printed paper if you are uncomfortable with the ink. Cannot be spot-cleaned.
Paper Towels	Safe, highly absorbent.	May be unattractive to some. Can be expensive for large cages or large collections. Cannot be spot-cleaned.
Commercial Paper Product	Safe and easy to maintain.	May be unattractive to some. Can be expensive with long term use. Cannot be spot-cleaned.
Aspen Shavings	Allows snake to burrow, easy to spot-clean.	May be ingested, messy, can be expensive. Rots if it becomes wet.
Pine Shavings	Allows snake to burrow, easy to spot-clean.	May be ingested, messy, can be expensive. Rots if it becomes wet.
Cypress Mulch	Allows snake to burrow, easy to spot-clean. Many find it attractive. Retains moisture well.	May be ingested, sharp sticks may harm snakes, messy, can be expensive.
Fir (Orchid) Bark	Allows snake to burrow, easy to spot-clean. Many find it attractive. Retains	May be ingested, messy, can be expensive.

	moisture well.	
Pulp Paper Products	Allows snake to burrow, easy to spot-clean.	May be unattractive to some. May be ingested, messy, can be expensive.

Chapter 14: Heating

Providing the proper thermal environment is one of the most important aspects of snake husbandry. As ectothermic ("cold blooded") animals, snakes rely on the local temperatures to regulate the rate at which their metabolism operates. Providing a proper thermal environment can mean the difference between keeping your pet healthy and spending your time at the veterinarian's office, battling infections and illness.

While there is variation from one form to the next, most kingsnakes require regular access to temperatures between 80 and 85 degrees Fahrenheit (26 to 30 degrees Celsius). However, they should not be kept at such temperatures constantly – snakes benefit from cooler nights and the ability to escape warm temperatures through the day.

1) Thermal Gradients

In the wild, a kingsnake spends much of its time moving between different microhabitats so that it can maintain its ideal temperature at the given time.

A kingsnake will crawl out on a warm, sunny rock to warm up in the morning, and retreat to a cool rodent burrow in the mid afternoon once the temperatures rise. As the sun approaches the horizon, the kingsnake may come out and move freely in the warm temperatures, and seek shelter once more when the temperatures drop too low.

You want to provide similar opportunities for captive snakes. While it is not possible to provide such a complex habitat in captivity, you should provide a thermal gradient, which is the next best thing.

To establish a thermal gradient, place the heating devices at one end of the habitat. This creates a basking spot, which should have the highest temperatures in the cage. This area should be larger than your snake's coiled body so that he can warm his entire body if he wishes.

Because there is no heat source at the other end of the cage, the temperature will gradually fall as your snake moves away from the heat source.

Ideally, the difference between the coolest spot in the cage and the basking spot will be at least 12 to 14 Fahrenheit (8 to 10 degrees Celsius), and larger if possible. If more than one heat source is required for the habitat, they should be clustered at one end.

The need to establish a thermal gradient is one of the most compelling reasons to use a large cage. In general, the larger the cage, the easier it is to establish a drastic thermal gradient.

2) Heat Lamps

Heat lamps are one of the best choices for supplying heat to kingsnakes. Heat lamps consist of a reflector dome and an incandescent bulb. The light bulb produces heat (in addition to light) and the metal reflector dome directs the heat to a spot inside the cage.

If you use a cage with a metal screen lid, you can rest the reflector dome directly on the screen; otherwise, you will need to clamp the lamp to something over the cage. Always be sure that the lamp is securely attached and will not be dislodged by vibration, children or pets. Always opt to purchase heavy-duty reflector domes with ceramic bases, rather than economy units with plastic bases.

While you can use specialized light bulbs that are designed for use with reptiles, it is not necessary. Regular, economy, incandescent bulbs work well. Snakes do not require special lighting, and incandescent bulbs – even those produced for use with reptiles – rarely generate much UVA, and never generate UVB.

One of the greatest benefits of using heat lamps to maintain the temperature of your snake's habitat is the inherent (and affordable) flexibility. While heat tapes and other devices are easy to adjust, a rheostat or thermostat is necessary to do so. Such devices are not prohibitively expensive, but they will raise the budget of your snake's habitat.

By contrast, heat lamps offer flexibility in two ways:

Changing the Bulb Wattage

The simplest way to adjust the temperature of your kingsnake's cage is by changing the wattage of the bulb being used. For example, if a 40-watt light bulb is not raising the temperature of the basking spot high enough, you may try a 60-watt bulb. Alternatively, if a 100-watt light bulb is elevating the cage temperatures higher than are appropriate, switching the bulb to a 60-watt model may help.

Adjusting the Height of the Heat Lamp

The closer the heat lamp is to the cage, the warmer the cage will be. Use this characteristic to your advantage. For example, if the habitat is too warm, the light can be raised, which should lower the cage temperatures slightly.

However, the higher the heat lamp is raised, the larger the basking spot becomes. Accordingly, it is important to be careful that you do not raise the light too high, which results in reducing the effectiveness of the cage's thermal gradient. In very large cages, this may not compromise the thermal gradient very much, but in a small cage, it may eliminate the "cool side" of the habitat.

In other words, if your heat lamp creates a basking spot that is roughly 1-foot in diameter when it rests directly on the screen, it may produce a slightly cooler, but larger basking spot when raised 6-inches above the level of the screen.

One way to avoid reducing the effectiveness of the gradient is through the use of "spot" bulbs, which produce a relatively narrow beam of light. Such lights may be slightly more expensive than economy bulbs, but because they make heat gradients easier to achieve, they deserve consideration.

One problem with using heat lamps is the current trend in which many manufacturers have stopped producing incandescent bulbs. In some municipalities, they may even be illegal to sell. It remains to be seen if incandescent bulbs will remain available to herpetoculturists over the long term or not. Fortunately, many other heating options are available.

3) Ceramic Heat Emitters

Ceramic heat emitters are small inserts that function similarly to light bulbs, except that they do not produce any visible light – they only produce heat.

Ceramic heat emitters are used in reflector-dome fixtures, just as heat lamps are. The benefits of such devices are numerous:

They typically last much longer than light bulbs do

They are suitable for use with thermostats

They allow for the creation of overhead basking spots, as lights do

They can be used day or night

However, the devices do have three primary drawbacks:

They are very hot when in operation

They are much more expensive than light bulbs

You cannot tell by looking if they are hot or cool. This can be a safety hazard – touching a ceramic heat emitter while it is hot is likely to cause serious burns.

Ceramic heat emitters are nearly the same price as radiant heat panels are. This causes many to select radiant heat panes over ceramic heat emitters. Radiant heat panels are generally preferable to ceramic heat emitters, as they usually have a light that indicates when they are on, and they do not get as hot on the surface.

4) Radiant Heat Panels

Quality radiant heat panels are the best choice for heating most reptile habitats, including those containing kingsnakes. Radiant heat panels are essentially heat pads that stick to the roof of the habitat. They usually feature rugged, plastic or metal casings and internal reflectors to direct the infrared heat back into the cage.

Radiant heat panels have a number of benefits over traditional heat lamps and under tank heat pads:

They do not contact the animal at all, thus reducing the risk of burns.

They do not produce visible light, which means they are useful for both diurnal and nocturnal heat production. They can be used in conjunction with fluorescent light fixtures during the day, and remain on at night once the lights go off.

They are inherently flexible. Unlike many devices that do not work well with pulse-proportional thermostats, most radiant heat panels work well with on-off and pulse-proportional thermostats.

The only real drawback to radiant heat panels is their cost: radiant heat panels often cost about two to three times the price of light- or heat pad-oriented systems. However, many radiant heat panels outlast light bulbs and heat pads, which offsets their high initial cost over the long term.

5) Heat Pads

Heat pads are an attractive option for many new keepers, but they are not without drawbacks.

Heat pads have a high risk for causing contact burns.

If they malfunction, they can damage the cage as well as the surface on which they are placed.

They are more likely to cause a fire than heat lamps or radiant heat panels are.

However, if installed properly (which includes allowing fresh air to flow over the exposed side of the heat pad) and used in conjunction with a thermostat, they can be reasonably safe. With heat pads, it behooves the keeper to purchase premium products, despite the small increase in price.

6) Heat Tape

Heat tape is somewhat akin to "stripped down" heat pads. In fact, most heat pads are simply pieces of heat tape that have already been connected and sealed inside a plastic envelope.

Heat tape is primarily used to heat large numbers of cages simultaneously. It is generally inappropriate for novices, and requires the keeper to make electrical connections. Additionally, a thermostat is always required when using heat tape.

Historically, heat tape was used to keep water pipes from freezing – not to heat reptile cages. While some commercial heat tapes have been designed specifically for reptiles, many have not. Accordingly, it may be illegal, not to mention dangerous, to use such heat tapes to heat reptile cages.

7) Heat Cables

Heat cables are similar to heat tape, in that they heat a long strip of the cage, but they are much more flexible and easy to use.

Many heat cables are suitable to use inside the cage, while others are designed for use outside the habitat.

Always be sure to purchase heat cables that are designed to be used in reptile cages. Those sold at hardware stores are not appropriate for use in a cage.

Heat cables must be used in conjunction with a thermostat, or, at the very least, a rheostat.

8) Hot Rocks

In the early days of commercial reptile products, faux rocks, branches and caves with internal heating elements were very popular. However, they have generally fallen out of favor among modern keepers. These rocks and branches were often made with poor craftsmanship and cheap materials, causing them to fail and produce tragic results. Additionally, many keepers used the rocks improperly, leading to injuries, illnesses and death for many unfortunate reptiles.

Heated rocks are not designed to heat an entire cage; they are designed to provide a localized source of heat for the reptile. Nevertheless, many keepers tried to use them as the primary heat source for the cage, resulting in dangerously cool cage temperatures.

While it is true that wild kingsnakes bask on rocks that have been warmed by the sun, the rock does not serve as the snake's only source of heat. When snakes must rely on small, localized heat sources placed in otherwise chilly cages, they often hug these heat sources for extended periods of time. This can lead to serious thermal burns – whether or not the units function properly. This illustrates the key reason why these devices make adequate supplemental heat sources, but they should not be used as primary heating sources.

Modern hot rocks utilize better features, materials and craftsmanship than the old models did, but they still offer few benefits to the keeper or the kept. Additionally, any heating devices that are designed to be used inside the cage necessitate passing an electric cable through a hole, which is not always easy to accomplish. However, some cages do feature passageways for chords.

9) Thermometers

It is important to monitor the cage temperatures very carefully to ensure your pet stays healthy. Just as a water test kit is an aquarist's best friend, a quality thermometer is one of the most important husbandry tools for snakes.

Ambient and Surface Temperatures

Two different types of temperature are relevant for pet snakes: ambient temperatures and surface temperatures.

The ambient temperature in your animal's cage is the air temperature. By contrast, surface temperatures are those of the objects in the cage.

For example, the air temperatures may be 90 degrees Fahrenheit (32 degrees Celsius) on a hot summer day. However, the black asphalt of the road may be much hotter than this. If you checked the surface temperatures of the road, they may be in excess of 120 degrees Fahrenheit (48 degrees Celsius).

In general, the ambient temperatures require more frequent monitoring and attention. As long as the surface temperatures of the cage do not exceed about 120 degrees Fahrenheit, your snake is not likely to be harmed from incidental contact. However, ambient temperatures of 120 degrees would be fatal very quickly.

Measure the cage's ambient temperatures with a digital thermometer. An indoor-outdoor model will feature a probe that allows you to measure the temperature at both ends of the thermal gradient at once. For example, you may have the thermometer positioned at the cool side of the cage, but the remote probe placed under the basking lamp.

Standard digital thermometers do not measure surface temperatures well. Instead, you should use a non-contact, infrared thermometer. Such devices will allow you to measure surface temperatures accurately and from a short distance away.

10) Thermostats and Rheostats

Some heating devices, such as heat lamps, are designed to operate at full capacity for the entire time that they are on. Such devices should not be used with thermostats – instead, care should be taken to calibrate the proper temperature.

Other devices, such as heat pads, heat tape and radiant heat panels are designed to be used with a regulating device to maintain the proper temperature, such as a thermostat or rheostat.

Rheostats

Rheostats are similar to light-dimmer switches, and they allow you to reduce the output of a heating device. In this way, you can dial in the proper temperature for the habitat.

The drawback to rheostats is that they only regulate the amount of power going to the device – they do not monitor the cage temperature or adjust the power flow automatically. In practice, even with the same level of power entering the device, the amount of heat generated by most heat sources will vary over the course of the day.

If you set the rheostat so that it keeps the cage at the right temperature in the morning, it may become too hot by the middle of the day. Conversely, setting the proper temperature during the middle of the day may leave the morning temperatures too cool.

Care must be taken to ensure that the rheostat controller is not inadvertently bumped or jostled, causing the temperature to rise or fall outside of healthy parameters.

Thermostats

Thermostats are similar to rheostats, except that they also feature a temperature probe that monitors the temperature in the cage (or under the basking source). This allows the thermostat to adjust the power going to the device as necessary to maintain a predetermined temperature.

For example, if you place the temperature probe under a basking spot powered by a radiant heat panel, the thermostat will keep the temperature relatively constant under the basking site.

There are two different types of thermostats:

On-Off Thermostats work by cutting the power to the device when the probe's temperature reaches a given temperature. For example, if the thermostat were set to 85 degrees Fahrenheit (29 degrees Celsius), the heating device would turn off whenever the temperature is this high or higher. When the temperature falls below 85, the thermostat will restore power to the unit, and the heater will begin functioning again. This cycle will repeat over and over again, thus maintaining the temperature within a relatively small range.

Be aware that on-off thermostats have a "lag" factor, meaning that they do not turn off when the temperature reaches a given temperature. They turn off when the temperature is a few degrees *above* that temperature, and then turn back on when the temperate is a little *below* the set point. Because of this, it is important to avoid setting the temperature at the limits of your pet's acceptable range. Some premium models have an adjustable amount of threshold for this factor, which is helpful.

Pulse proportional thermostats work by constantly sending pulses of electricity to the heater. By varying the rate of pulses, the amount of energy reaching the heating devices varies. A small computer inside the thermostat adjusts this rate to match the set-point temperature as measured by the probe. Accordingly, pulse proportional thermostats maintain much more consistent temperatures than on-off thermostats do.

Lights should not be used with thermostats, as the constant flickering may stress your snake. Conversely, heat pads, heat tape, radiant heat panels and ceramic heat emitters should always be used with either a rheostat or, preferably, a thermostat to avoid overheating your snake.

Thermostat Failure

If used for long enough, all thermostats eventually fail – the question is, will yours fail today or twenty years from now? While some thermostats fail in the "off" position, a thermostat that fails in the "on" position may overheat your snakes. Unfortunately, tales of entire collections being lost to a faulty thermostat are too common.

Accordingly, it behooves the keeper to acquire high-quality thermostats. Some keepers use two thermostats, connected in series arrangement. By setting the second thermostat (the "backup thermostat") a few degrees higher than the setting used on the "primary thermostat," you safeguard yourself against the failure of either unit.

In such a scenario, the backup thermostat allows the full power coming to it to travel through to the heating device, as the temperature never reaches its higher set-point temperature. However, if the first unit fails in the "on" position, the second thermostat will keep the temperatures from becoming too high. The temperature will rise a few degrees in accordance with the higher set-point temperature, but it will not get hot enough to harm your snakes.

If the backup thermostat fails in the "on" position, the first thermostat should still retain control. If either fails in the "off" position, the temperature will fall until you rectify the situation, but a brief exposure to relatively cool temperatures is unlikely to be fatal.

11) Nighttime Heating

In most circumstances, you should provide your kingsnake with a 10 to 20 degree temperature drop at night. Some keepers achieve success with constant heat, but wild kingsnakes are almost invariably exposed to such temperature fluctuations, which may provide some benefits.

Most people keep their houses sufficiently warm at night to allow a pet kingsnake's cage to drop to room temperature. To do so, you can simply switch your heating device off at night, and turn it back on in the morning. Alternatively, you can plug the heating devices (and thermostats or rheostats) into a lamp-timer to automate the process. Some thermostats have features that adjust the temperature of the thermostat during the night, lowering it to a specified level.

Others, who must provide some type of nocturnal heat source for their pet, can do so in a number of ways. Virtually any non-light-emitting heat source will function adequately in this capacity. Ceramic heating elements, radiant heat panels and heat pads, cables and tape all work well for supplying nocturnal heat.

Red lights can be used in reflector domes to provide heat as well. In fact, red lights can be used for day and night heating, but the cage will not be illuminated very well, unless other lights are incorporated during the day.

12) Incorporating Thermal Mass

One underutilized technique that is helpful for making small changes in the way you heat a cage is by raising the cage's thermal mass. Rocks, large water dishes and ceramic cage decorations are examples of items that may work in such a context. These objects will absorb heat from the heat source, and then re-radiate heat into the habitat.

This changes the thermal characteristics of the habitat greatly. Often, keepers in cool climates benefit from these techniques when trying to warm cages sufficiently. By simply adding a large rock, the cage may eventually warm up a few degrees.

For kingsnakes, rocks or clean bricks are the best, as a large water dish may raise the humidity level too much for these species.

Raising the cage's thermal mass also helps reduce the cage's rate of cooling in the evening. By placing a thick rock under the basking light, it will absorb heat all day and re-radiate this heat after the lights turn off. Eventually it will reach room temperature, but this may take hours.

Always remember to monitor the cage surface temperatures and ambient temperatures regularly after changing the thermal characteristics of the cage. Pay special attention to the surface temperatures of items placed on or under a heat source.

Experiment with different amounts of thermal mass in the cage. Use items of different sizes, shapes and materials, and see how the cage temperatures change. In general, the more thermal mass in the cage, the more constant the temperature will stay.

However, this may not always be desirable. Consider a keeper living in south Florida, with a pet California mountain kingsnake (*Lampropeltis zonata*). California kingsnakes appreciate significant nighttime temperature drops, and it is all the Florida-based keeper's home air-conditioning unit can do to drop the temperature to 72 degrees Fahrenheit (22 degrees Celsius) at night. Such a keeper must maximize all of the daily temperature fluctuation he can, by cooling the cage off as quickly as possible each night.

By contrast, a keeper living in Sweden who keeps a Louisiana Milksnake (*Lampropeltis triangulum amaura*) is trying to keep the cage temperature from falling too far at night, or drying out too much from evaporative cooling. Such a keeper may benefit significantly from adding thermal mass to the cage.

13) Room Heat

Some keepers with very large collections elect to heat the entire room, rather than individual cages. While this is an economic and viable solution for advanced keepers, it is not appropriate for novices.

Heating the whole room, instead of an individual cage, makes it very difficult to achieve a good thermal gradient. Experienced keepers may be able to maintain their snakes successfully in this manner, but beginners should always rely on the added safety afforded by a gradient.

Additionally, room heat is rarely cost-effective for a keeper with a pet snake or two. Relying on a single heating source for an entire room is also a high-risk proposition; if the heater or thermostat fails in the "on" position, the entire room may overheat.

14) Maintaining Your Snake at Room Temperature

Some keepers and breeders advocate keeping some kingsnakes at or near room temperature. While this is possible in some very select circumstances, the endeavor is wrought with the potential for catastrophe.

While some snakes, such as Eastern milk snakes (*Lampropeltis triangulum triangulum*), may normally live at temperatures comparable to those of some homes, they do use the environment to heat up when digesting their food or battling infection.

Preventing them from accessing suitable basking sites is a bad idea, especially for new keepers.

Chapter 15: Lighting

Kingsnakes do not require special or elaborate lighting. Heat lamps provide plenty of illumination for them, while ambient light that enters their cage is sufficient for cages that do not use heat lamps for warmth. However, some keepers prefer to incorporate supplemental lighting to improve the visibility of their snake.

Fluorescent bulbs are the best choice for supplemental lighting. These lights produce light of higher quality than incandescent bulbs do, and they do not produce very much heat.

Full-spectrum lights with a high color-rendering index will make your snake look his best, but even economy bulbs will allow you to see your animal better. Reptile-specific lights are not required for kingsnakes, as they do not require exposure to ultraviolet radiation to metabolize their dietary calcium and vitamin D, as many lizards and turtles do.

If you choose to employ cage lighting, keep your species habitat preferences in mind to ensure the light levels are appropriate. For example, forms that inhabit wide-open deserts or grasslands are likely to be more comfortable with bright lights than those that inhabit relatively dimly lit forests.

Additionally, it is important to cycle the cage lights in such a way that replicates natural photoperiods. Constant lighting is likely to stress the snake, while insufficient hours of daylight may cause them to initiate brumating behaviors. Plug the lights into a lamp timer to ensure a consistent photoperiod.

If you do not intend to breed your kingsnake, you do not have to provide him with a yearly photo cycle – you can leave the lights on for 12 hours each day, year round. However, snakes that are designated to be breed must have seasonally appropriate photoperiods throughout the year.

If heat lamps are used to keep the nighttime temperatures from dropping too low, be sure to use red lights, which are not likely to disrupt the snake's day-night cycle.

Just as you provide a thermal gradient for your snake, ideally, you should provide a photo gradient as well. This will allow the snake to move between dark and light areas, which further replicates his natural lifestyle.

Always measure the cage temperatures after adding or changing the type of light sources used. While fluorescent lights do not produce a lot of heat, they may generate enough to warm small cages to undesirable levels.

Chapter 16: Handling and Transport

One of the most enjoyable aspects of snake keeping for many people is handling their pet. While most kingsnakes will learn to accept regular, gentle handling, proper technique will make handling time more enjoyable for you and less stressful for your pet.

Picking up a Snake

Learning to pick up a snake correctly is easy, and will often yield positive results, as it starts handling sessions on the right track.

Ensure the surroundings are conducive to snake handling. Do not pick up snakes (unless necessary) when pets, children or other potential distractions are nearby.

Open the cage or take off the lid.

Immediately scoop your hand under the snake and gently lift him around the middle of his body.

With your other hand, support the rest of his body and remove him from the cage.

Do not stand in front of the cage for extended periods of time, trying to gather the nerve to pick up your snake. This often makes snakes nervous. The goal is for your snake to learn to anticipate the activity and react calmly.

If the snake shows signs of aggression, you should remain deliberate and calm. Many young kingsnakes are feisty as youngsters, but their strikes and bites are harmless. With repeated handling sessions, such snakes usually become considerably tamer.

It is important to consider that some snakes may never become tractable, trustworthy pets. You will still need to care for your snake if this happens, and you need to have a plan of action for doings so.

Many advanced keepers would simply proceed as usual, and simply endure the mildly irritating bites and musking. But beginners will often feel more comfortable using alternative methods for handling such snakes.

How to Hold a Snake

When holding a snake, avoid restraining it. Instead, seek to support its body weight, and allow it to crawl from one hand to the other. Kingsnakes do not usually grip their handler with their tail, so be careful not to drop your pet. It is always wise to handle the snake over a table or other object to prevent his from falling to the floor, should he make a sudden move.

Always realize that you are responsible for your snake while you are holding it. While bites from even a large kingsnake usually only result in minor injuries, accidents can happen. Such occurrences are very bad for snakes, snake keepers and the entire snake-keeping hobby, and must be avoided. Never handle your snake in a public situation.

Do not take your snake to the park or to the local fast food restaurant. He is not a toy, he does not appreciate "hanging out" in this manner, and it makes snake keepers everywhere look bad.

Snakes frighten many people and you should always be sensitive to this fact. Rather than playing into these fears, seek to educate people about snakes rather than shock them by bringing them to inappropriate events and locations.

Dealing with Aggressive Snakes

Fortunately, many kingsnakes are calm and docile serpents. However, some will bite when frightened. Although patience and calm, deliberate care may reduce these aggressive tendencies, some snakes may remain aggressive for their entire life.

If you can resign yourself to having a "look but don't touch" snake, then you can avoid most problems associated with such animals. When you do need to move your aggressive snake, you can do so by using a "transfer box," instead of your hands.

Simply open his cage, and scoop him into a plastic storage box. If you do this quickly, deliberately and gently, he will gradually learn to anticipate the activity and it will get easier. Place the lid on the box and set the entire box to the side while you tend to his cage.

Another idea is to devise a cover for the opening to one of his favorite hiding spots. This way, when you need to tend to the cage, you can simply wait for him to enter the hide and cover the opening. The hide box can then be moved to wherever you need it to go.

You can also acquire and learn to use a snake hook to move your animal. Doing so takes some practice, and you must be careful not to let the snake fall from the hook and hurt himself. Use the smallest hook you can (many manufacturers make small "cage hooks" specifically for this purpose) and learn to move him back and forth with precision.

Finally, though many do not have the stomach for it, you can simply pick the snake up with your hands. Often, you will find that the snake would rather protest, hiss, musk and rattle his tail than actually bite.

If you like, a pair of gloves and a long sleeve shirt will provide rather effective "armor" for dealing with your angry beast.

Do take care to avoid allowing the snake to get close to your face; a nip here could be more serious.

In The Event of a Bite

Kingsnakes have relatively weak jaws and small mouths, which makes most bites insignificant occurrences. A tangle with a rose bush is far more painful and troubling than a nip from a 3-foot-long kingsnake.

Most non-defensive bites from kingsnakes arise from feeding mistakes. Some kingsnakes are such aggressive feeders that they will bite anything that smells, moves or tastes like food. Accordingly, it is best to wash your hands before handling your snake to ensure that your hands do not smell of potential prey. This is especially important for keepers who have other pet snakes or lizards.

If a kingsnake actually bites you, it is likely to hold on until it realizes that you are not appropriate food. If you like, you can simply endure the very slight amount of pain from the snake's tiny teeth until he lets go. This is the least traumatic way to get the snake to release its grip, however, there are other, quicker, methods available.

One relatively safe way to get a snake to release its grip is to plunge your hand and the snake into a bucket of cold water. If this does not work, an alcohol-soaked cotton swab held in front of the snake's nose and mouth will usually get them to release.

If none of these techniques work, you can try to pry the snake's mouth off your hand, but you must do so carefully to avoid exacerbating your injury or harming the snake's teeth or mouth.

Try to slide a thin piece of cardboard or plastic (such as a credit card) in the snake's mouth. Do so very gently and slowly. Many times, the snake will release his grip in an attempt to achieve a better bite. When this happens, push the card back further to prevent the teeth from penetrating your skin again. You can use gentle pressure to encourage the snake to release its grip.

Once you have removed the snake, return him to his cage and allow him to rest (it is a high-stress event for him too!). Wash the wound with soap and water, and apply an antibiotic medication to the wound.

While most (non-venomous) snake bites heal with little consequence, consult your doctor if the area exhibits signs of infection, such as red color, inflammation or discharge.

Temporary Transport Cages

The best way to transport your snake is with a plastic storage container. The container must have ample air holes to allow ventilation and it must be safe and secure.

Some keepers prefer transparent boxes for such purposes, as they allow you to see the snake while it is inside the box. This is definitely a benefit – especially when opening and closing the box – but opaque transportation boxes provide your snake with more security, as they cannot see the activity going on outside their container.

Place a few paper towels or some clean newspaper in the bottom of the box to give your snake somewhere to hide and to absorb any fluids, should your snake defecate or discharge urates.

Transporting Tips

When traveling with your snake, pay special attention to the temperature. Use the air-conditioning or heater in your vehicle to keep the snake within his comfortable range (the mid-70s Fahrenheit are ideal in most circumstances).

Do not jostle your snake unnecessarily, nor leave it unattended in a car. Make sure that the transport container is secure – in the unfortunate circumstance in which you are in an accident, a loose snake is not an additional problem with which you need to contend.

Hygiene

Always practice good hygiene when handling snakes. Wash your hands with soap and warm water each time you touch your snake, his habitat or the tools you use to care for him.

Never wash cages or tools in kitchens or bathrooms that are used by humans.

Chapter 17: Breeding

Many snake keepers are intrigued at the idea of breeding their snakes. While this is a fun, educational activity, you must be sure that you understand the risks and responsibilities that accompany such attempts.

For example, it is often necessary to allow your snake to brumate to instigate breeding behaviors. Exposing your animal to reduced temperatures makes them more susceptible to illness. When their body temperatures are low, snakes' immune systems do not work as effectively as normal. If your snakes become sick during the brumation period, they will require immediate veterinary attention.

Additionally, anytime two kingsnakes are housed together, there is the risk that one will try to eat the other. Even if the larger snake is not able to consume the smaller, it is likely to kill the smaller snake while constricting it. This potential is higher for the forms that routinely eat snakes, such as those of the *getula*-complex, such as eastern, speckled and California kingsnakes. These risks are much lower with other forms, such as scarlet kingsnakes and many milksnakes.

Other problems may occur as well; males may suffer damaged hemipenes or females may become egg bound. Either of which may be fatal without prompt treatment. You may find it necessary to take your pet to the veterinarian for costly treatment – potentially without any guarantee of success.

If you manage to get through the entire process without problem, you will one day find eggs that require incubation. If this is successful, you will find yourself caring for a dozen or more other snakes. While it is possible to sell them, this is not as easy as it sounds, and rarely generates profit.

Many municipalities require expensive permits to keep large numbers of snakes – selling them requires other permits altogether. You will have to learn how to ship snakes and obtain the necessary permits for that. Additionally, you will have to spend money to advertise that you have snakes for sale. Ultimately, most beginners find that it is simply best to give away the snakes to prospective keepers.

One of the biggest challenges to breeding kingsnakes is convincing the resulting youngsters to feed. Most hatchling kingsnakes consume lizards in the wild. As wild caught lizards are likely to be parasitized and unsuitable for your hatchlings and captive produced lizards are not economically viable, it is necessary to convince them to eat neonatal rodents.

While hobbyists are often successful at convincing a single pet snake to begin eating rodents, it is rare for a hobbyist to succeed with an entire clutch of hatchling kingsnakes. This may necessitate tube feedings or other drastic measures.

Finally, you must consider the costs associated with housing a large number of hatchlings. Each will need its own habitat, heat supply and water dish, as they cannot be housed together.

1) Pre-Cycling Conditioning

Only snakes in perfect health should be considered for breeding trials. If a snake exhibits signs of stress, respiratory illness, mites, mouth rot or other illnesses, avoid breeding the snake or engaging in cycling until the snake is 100 percent health.

During the late summer and early fall, feed adults slated for breeding trials heavily. However, avoid allowing either animal to become overweight – overweight snakes make poor breeders.

Thermal- and Photo-Cycling

By late autumn, while the cage temperatures are still at their normal levels, stop feeding the snakes. After at least two weeks have passed, and the snakes have had time to empty their digestive system completely, you can gradually begin lowering the cage temperature. It can also be helpful to reduce the relatively day-length, as happens in the wild.

After two to four weeks of lowering the temperature, you can place the snake in a full state of brumation, with temperatures of approximately 55 to 65 degrees Fahrenheit (12 to 18 degrees Celsius), depending on the species.

Most often, this entails turning the heating devices off completely and allowing the temperatures to fall. Usually the snakes will become essentially dormant, although they may move about from time to time, drink water or respond to stimuli.

The proper temperatures for brumation vary from one species to the next, but generally correspond with the winter temperatures in the species' homeland. For example, Florida kingsnakes (*Lampropeltis floridana*) require only a very mild brumation period, and may even breed without cycling. By comparison, Pale milksnakes (*Lampropeltis triangulum multistrata*) – especially specimens from the northern part of their range – may require long, cold, dark brumation periods to spur breeding activity.

Often, it is necessary to move the cage (or use a separate brumation container) to another location to achieve the proper temperatures. For instance, garages, storage rooms and other places may dip into the 50s Fahrenheit, offering more appropriate temperatures than a living room or bedroom.

The length of brumation varies, but in general, two months is the approximate amount of time necessary. After this, you can gradually increase the temperatures until they are back to normal.

Once your snakes have been warm for a few days, you can consider feeding them, although many will refuse food.

2) Pairing

As soon as the snakes have been brought back up to the correct temperatures, they are ready to begin introducing to each other.

It is always wise to observe snakes when you introduce them to each other – particularly when it is the first time two snakes have met. Some snakes just are not compatible, and may engage in antagonistic behaviors or fight. This can lead to serious injuries or death if the subordinate animal cannot escape. Further, kingsnakes are always at risk for consuming cage mates.

Some breeders prefer to place males in the females' cages, while others prefer the opposite. Still others use a neutral cage, unique to both.

Pairs may begin copulating minutes after you place them in the same cage, or they may never breed if they are not compatible. Generally, snakes are housed together until they copulate, and then they are separated and fed, if they will eat.

Reintroduce the snakes periodically to allow further matings and increase the chances for fertile eggs. When the pair stops showing interest, halt the introductions.

It is important to note that female kingsnakes can produce clutches that were sired by multiple fathers. While this has been demonstrated in laboratory conditions, it remains unclear how often this occurs in the wild. (R. G. Zweifel, 1983)

3) Post-Partum Care and Egg Deposition

After several copulations, the female can be kept by herself and fed regularly. Always offer smaller-than-normal food items at this time, to reduce the chances of disrupting the reproductive processes. However, feed fully furred rodents to females to ensure they get enough calcium (via the rodent's bones, which are much more substantial in size by the time the rodent has developed fur).

A few weeks after successful mating, the female with ovulate. Snakes have two ovaries, which may release ova at the same time or individually, a few days apart. When snakes ovulate, all of the ova in a given ovary are released simultaneously, allowing them to move into the oviducts, where they are shelled and eventually deposited a few weeks later.

Ovulation may create a dramatic mid-body swelling in the female. It can be much larger than the bulge caused by a typical food item, or it can be small enough to go unnoticed. However, ovulation marks an important reference point when trying to prepare for the ensuing eggs.

Most snakes shed once between the time of ovulation and egg deposition. About two to four weeks after this shed (depending on the species); the female will deposit the eggs. Accordingly, you must provide her with an egg-laying box when she is about to shed.

The egg-laying box is similar to a hide box, but it includes some moss, mulch or newspaper in the bottom. Different breeders prefer different substrates for the box, but there is likely little difference between the various options.

The egg-laying medium should be very slightly damp, but not wet. Err on the side of dryness, to avoid problems with mold, bacteria and fungi.

Once the female has finished depositing the eggs, she will often leave them, as kingsnakes do not practice any maternal care. You can generally reach in the cage and remove the entire egg box at this point.

Allow the female to rest and rehydrate for about 24 hours, and then offer her food. Most females eat ravenously at this time to help replenish their energy stores.

4) Incubation

Most breeders incubate kingsnake eggs inside a climate-controlled box, known as an incubator. The eggs are generally arranged in small plastic boxes containing an incubation medium, and the boxes are then placed inside the incubation chamber.

A thermostat keeps the temperature correct, while the humidity of the box is controlled by adding water to the substrate as needed.

Plastic storage boxes are often used for egg incubation. Fill the box half way with damp vermiculite. Ensure that the vermiculite is damp enough to clump, but not so damp that it drips when compressed. As a starting point, combine equal weights of water and vermiculite and then adjust the mixture as necessary. Make a few small holes in the incubation box to provide some air exchange.

Before removing the eggs from the egg-laying box, mark the top of each egg with a graphite pencil. This is necessary because the tiny snake embryo attaches to the inside of the eggshell at an early stage in development. If the egg is rotated after this happens, the young animal can drown inside the egg.

After marking the tops, gently remove the eggs and transfer them to the egg incubation box. Do not use force to separate any eggs that are attached – while experienced breeders often separate such eggs, the risk of destroying some of them is high. Simply place clumps of attached eggs in the egg incubation box in the same orientation in which they are in the deposition box.

Place the eggs in the incubation box in the same orientation in which they were deposited in the egg-laying box. Bury the eggs about halfway in the vermiculite.

There are many different opinions regarding the best place to install the thermostat's temperature probe. Some prefer placing it in the main incubator chamber, while others prefer to place the probe inside the egg box.

Place the egg incubation box inside the incubator and close it tightly. Do not inspect the eggs too frequently, as this may cause unnecessary temperature spikes.

Most kingsnake eggs hatch in 60 to 65 days, depending on the species and incubation temperature. You can incubate most kingsnake eggs at about 80 degrees Fahrenheit (26 degrees Celsius).

5) Hatchling Husbandry

Establish "nursery cages" for the young snakes about a week before the eggs should hatch. Some keepers house their hatchlings together until their first shed, but this courts disaster.

The container should contain only a paper towel substrate, a very shallow water dish, and some places to hide (crumpled newspaper works well).

Keep the nursery very clean, slightly humid and at about 80 degrees Fahrenheit (26 degrees Celsius), 24-hours a day. The hatchlings do not need much light – that coming in the side of the nursery is ample.

Do not handle the hatchlings unless necessary, until they are about one month old and eating well.

It is not uncommon for hatchlings to emerge with their yolks still attached. Do not attempt to remove or separate the tissue in such situations; doing so could cause severe injury or death to the hatchling. Instead, simply keep the hatchling in a nursery cage and ensure that the tissue does not dry out. Generally, by keeping the nursery slightly humid, the tissue will remain moist and dethatch on in its own in a few days.

Hatchlings shed about one week after they hatch. At this point, you can place them in habitats that are like small versions of the adult cages.

Give them a few days to settle in, and begin offering food. Some experienced keepers prefer to offer food as soon as possible after shedding, but others prefer to wait. In either case, your snake has energy reserves that will sustain them for several weeks, so there is no need to rush the process.

Chapter 18: Veterinary Care and Health Problems

Unlike humans, who can tell you when they are sick, snakes endure illness stoically. This does not mean that injury or illnesses do not cause them distress, but without expressive facial features, they do not look like they are suffering.

In fact, many snake illnesses do not produce symptoms until the disease has already reached an advanced state. Accordingly, it is important to treat injuries and illness promptly to provide your pet with the best chance of recovery.

1) Finding a Suitable Veterinarian

Relatively few veterinarians treat snakes and other reptiles. It is important to find a snake-oriented veterinarian before you need one. There are a number of ways to do this:

You can search veterinarian databases to find one that is local and treats reptiles.

You can inquire with your dog or cat veterinarian to see if he or she knows a qualified reptile-oriented veterinarian to whom he or she can refer you.

You can contact a local reptile-enthusiast group or club. Most such organizations will be familiar with the local veterinarians.

You can inquire with local nature preserves or zoos. Most such institutions have relationships with veterinarians that treat reptiles and other exotic animals.

If you happen to live in a remote area and do not have a reptile-oriented veterinarian within driving distance, you can try to find a conventional veterinarian who will treat your animal after consulting with a reptile-oriented veterinarian. Such visits may be expensive, as you will have to pay for two veterinary visits (the actual visit and the phone consultation), but it may be your only choice.

2) Reasons to Visit the Veterinarian

While snakes do not require vaccinations or similar routine treatments, they may require visits for other reasons. Anytime your snake exhibits signs of illness or suffers an injury, you must visit the veterinarian.

Visit your veterinarian when:

You first acquire your snake. This will allow your veterinarian to familiarize himself or herself with your pet while it is presumably healthy. This gives him or her a baseline against which he or she can consider future deviations. Additionally, your veterinarian may be able to diagnose existing illnesses, before they cause serious problems.

Any time your snake wheezes, exhibits labored breathing or produces a mucus discharge from its nostrils or mouth.

Anytime your snake produces soft or watery feces. (Soft feces is expected when snakes are fed some food items, such as birds. This is not necessarily cause for concern).

Any significant injury. Common examples include thermal burns, friction damage to the rostral (nose) region or damaged scales.

Reproductive issues, such as egg binding. If a snake appears nervous, agitated or otherwise stressed and unable to deposit her eggs, see your veterinarian immediately.

Long-term anorexia. While many snakes fast from time to time – which is no cause for concern – snakes that do not eat for 4 weeks should be seen by a veterinarian.

3) Common Health Problems

Some of the common health problems, their causes and suggested course of action follow.

Retained or Poor Sheds

Captive snakes – especially in the hands of novice keepers – often shed poorly. With proper husbandry, healthy snakes should produce one-piece sheds regularly (if the shed skin is broken in one or two places, but comes off easily, there is no cause for concern.)

Retained sheds can cause health problems, particularly if they restrict blood flow. This is often a problem when a snake retains a bit of old skin near the tail tip.

If your snake sheds poorly, you must take steps to remove the old skin and review your husbandry to prevent the problem from happening again. If you are providing ideal husbandry parameters, and yet your snake still experiences poor sheds, consult your veterinarian to rule out illness.

The best way to remove retained sheds is by soaking your snake or placing him in a damp container for about an hour. After removing him, see if you can gently peel the skin off. Try to keep the skin in as few pieces as possible to make the job easier.

Do not force the skin off your snake. If it does not come off easily, return him to his cage and repeat the process again in 12 to 24 hours. Usually, repeated soaks or time in a damp hide will loosen the skin sufficiently to be removed.

If repeated treatments do not yield results, consult your veterinarian. He may feel that the retained shed is not causing a problem, and advise you to simply leave it attached – it should come off with the snake's next shed. Alternatively, it if is causing a problem, the veterinarian can remove it without much risk of harming your snake.

Retained Spectacles

Unlike a simple retained shed, a retained spectacle (eye cap) is a serious matter. Do not try to remove a retained spectacle yourself; simply keep the snake in a humid environment and take it to your veterinarian, who should be able to remove it relatively easily.

Respiratory Infections

Like humans, snakes can suffer from respiratory infections. Snakes with respiratory infections exhibit fluid or mucus draining from their nose and/or mouth, may be lethargic and are unlikely to eat. They may also spend excessive amounts of time basking on or under the heat source, in an effort to induce a "behavioral fever."

Bacteria, or, less frequently, fungi or parasites often cause respiratory infections. In addition, cleaning products, perfumes, pet dander and other particulate matter can irritate a snake's respiratory tract as well. Some such bacteria are ubiquitous, and only become problematic when they overwhelm a snake's immune system. Other bacteria (and most viruses) are transmitted from one snake to another.

To reduce the chances of illnesses, keep your snake quarantined from other snakes, keep his enclosure exceptionally clean and be sure to provide the best husbandry possible, in terms of temperature and humidity. Additionally, avoid stressing your snake by handling him too frequently, or exposing him to chaotic situations.

Upon taking your snake to the vet, he or she will likely take samples of the mucus and have them analyzed to determine the causal agent. The veterinarian will then prescribe medications, if appropriate, such as antibiotics.

It is imperative to carry out the actions prescribed by your veterinarian exactly as stated, and keep your snake's stress level very low while he is healing. Stress can reduce immune function, so avoid handling him unnecessarily, and consider covering the front of his cage while he recovers.

Many snakes produce audible breathing sounds for a few days immediately preceding a shed cycle. This is rarely cause for concern and will resolve once the snake sheds. However, if you are in doubt, always seek veterinary attention.

"Mouth Rot"

Mouth rot – properly called stomatitis – is identified by noting discoloration, discharge or cheesy-looking material in the snake's mouth. Mouth rot can be a serious illness, and requires the attention of your veterinarian.

While mouth rot can follow an injury (such as happens when a snake strikes the side of a glass cage) it can also arise from systemic illness. Your veterinarian will cleanse your snake's mouth and potentially prescribe an antibiotic.

Your veterinarian may recommend withholding food until the problem is remedied. Always be sure that snakes recovering from mouth rot have immaculately clean habitats, with ideal temperatures.

Internal Parasites

In the wild, most snakes carry some internal parasites. While it may not be possible to keep a snake completely free of internal parasites, it is important to keep these levels in check.

Consider any wild-caught snake to be parasitized until proven otherwise. While most captive bred snakes should have relatively few internal parasites, they can suffer from such problems as well.

Preventing parasites from building to pathogenic levels requires strict hygiene. Many parasites build up to dangerous levels when the snakes are kept in a cage that is continuously contaminated from feces.

Most internal parasites that are of importance for snakes are transmitted via the fecal-oral route. This means that eggs (or a similar life stage) of the parasites are released with the feces. If the snake inadvertently ingests these, the parasites can develop inside the snake's body and cause increased problems. Such eggs are usually microscopic and easily lifted into the air, where they may stick to cage walls or land in the water dish. Later, when the snake flicks its tongue or drinks from the water dish, it ingests the eggs.

Internal parasites may cause your snake to vomit, pass loose stools, fail to grow or refuse food entirely. Other parasites may produce no symptoms at all, demonstrating the importance of routine examinations.

Your veterinarian will usually examine your snake's feces if he suspects internal parasites. By looking at the type of eggs inside the snake's feces, you veterinarian can prescribe an appropriate medication. Many parasites are easily treated with anti-parasitic medications, but often, these medications must be given several times to completely eradicate the pathogens.

Some parasites may be transmissible to people, so always take proper precautions, including regular hand washing and keeping snakes and their cages away from kitchens and other areas where foods are prepared.

Examples of common internal parasites include roundworms, tapeworms and amoebas.

External Parasites

The primary external parasites that afflict snakes are ticks and snake mites. Ticks are rare on captive bred animals, but wild caught snakes often have a few.

Ticks should be removed manually. Using tweezers grasp the tick as close as possible to the snake's skin and pull with steady, gentle pressure. Do not place anything over the tick first, such as petroleum jelly, or carry out any other "home remedies," such as

123

burning the tick with a match. Such techniques may cause the tick to inject more saliva (which may contain diseases or bacteria) into the snake's body.

Drop the tick in a jar of isopropyl alcohol to ensure it is killed. It is a good idea to bring these to your veterinarian for analysis. Do not contact ticks with your bare hands, as many species can transmit disease to humans.

Mites are another matter entirely. While ticks are generally large enough to see easily, mites are about the size of a pepper flake. Whereas tick infestations usually only tally a few individuals, mite infestations may include thousands of individual parasites.

Mites may afflict wild caught snakes, but, as they are not confined to a small cage, such infestations are somewhat self-limiting. However, in captivity, mite infestations can approach plague proportions.

After a female mite feeds on a snake, she drops off and finds a safe place (such as a tiny crack in a cage or among the substrate) to deposit her eggs. After the eggs hatch, they travel back to your snake (or to other snakes in your collection) where they feed and perpetuate the lifecycle.

Whereas a few mites may represent little more than an inconvenience to the snake, a significant infection stresses them considerably, and may even cause death through anemia. This is particularly true for small or young animals. Additionally, mites may transmit disease from one snake to another.

There are a number of different methods for eradicating a mite infestation. In each, there are two primary steps that must be taken: the snake must be rid of the parasites, and the environment (which may include the room in which the cage resides) must be rid of the parasites as well.

It is relatively simple to remove mites from a snake. When mites get wet, they die. However, mites are protected by a thick, waxy exoskeleton that encourages the formation of an air bubble. This means that you cannot place your snake in water to drown the mites. The mites will simply hide under the snake's scales, using their air bubble to protect themselves.

To defeat this waxy cuticle, all that is needed is a few drops of gentle dish soap added to the water. The soap will lower the surface tension of water, allowing it to penetrate under the snake's scales. Additionally, the soap disrupts the surface tension of the water, preventing the air bubble from forming.

By soaking your snake is the slightly soapy water for about one hour will kill most of the mites on his body. Use care when doing so, but try to arrange the water level and container so that most of the snake's body is below the water.

While the snake is soaking, perform a thorough cage cleaning. Remove everything from the cage, including water dishes, substrates and cage props. Sterilize all impermeable cage items, and discard the substrate and all porous cage props. Vacuum the area around the cage and wipe down all of the nearby surfaces with a wet cloth.

It may be necessary to repeat this process several times to eradicate the mites completely. Accordingly, the very best strategy is to avoid contracting mites in the first place. This is why it is important to purchase your snake from a reliable breeder or retailer, and keep your snake quarantined from potential mite vectors.

As an example, even if you purchase your snake from a reliable source, provide excellent husbandry and clean the cage regularly, you can end up battling mites if your friend brings his snake – which has a few mites – to your house.

It may be possible for mites to crawl onto your hands or clothes, hop off when you return home and make their way to your snake. This is why many breeders and experienced hobbyists avoid visiting low-quality pet stores or places with poorly tended snake cages.

While it is relatively easy to observe mites on a snake that has a significant infestation, a few mites may go unnoticed. Make it a practice to inspect your snake and his cage regularly. Look in the crease under the snake's lower jaw, near the eyes and near the vent; all of these are places in which mites hide. It can also be helpful to wipe down your snake with a damp, white paper towel. After wiping down the snake, observe the towel to see if any mites are present.

Chemical treatments are also available to combat mites, but you must be very careful with such substances. Beginners should rely on their veterinarian to prescribe or suggest the appropriate chemicals.

Avoid repurposing lice treatments or other chemicals, as is often encouraged by other hobbyists. Such non-intended use may be very dangerous, and it is often in violation of Federal laws.

Generally speaking, new hobbyists should consult with their veterinarian if they suspect that their snake has mites. Mite eradication is often a challenging ordeal that your veterinarian can help make easier.

Dystocia (Egg-Binding)

Occasionally, female snakes exhibit problems depositing their eggs. Such a condition – termed dystocia – is a medical emergency. Without veterinary assistance, the snake is likely to die.

If your snake exhibits nervousness, pacing or starts depositing eggs and then stops (with eggs still visible within her body) take her to the veterinarian immediately.

Veterinarians can take a number of steps to resolve the situation. In the best-case scenario, an injection of calcium may resolve the issue.

Sometimes, one egg is simply too big to pass through the snake's cloaca. When this occurs, it may be possible for the vet to use a syringe to remove some of the fluid from inside the problem egg. This causes the egg to collapse and pass easily.

In worst-case scenarios, surgery is required. In some cases, the surgery will require the removal of the oviducts, which will render the female unable to breed in the future.

In all cases, retained eggs are highly unlikely to survive. By the time the eggs are ready to be deposited, they are running out of oxygen, and must be expelled so that they can absorb fresh air.

There are many reasons why a snake may become egg bound. Sometimes it is because the female did not have adequate energy reserves or enough dietary calcium. In other cases, it may just be bad luck. Reduce the chances of this happening by only allowing females to breed if they are in perfect health.

Long-Term Anorexia

While short-term fasts of one to two weeks are common among snakes, fasts that last longer than this may be cause for concern. If your snake refuses food, ensure that its habitat is set up ideally with ample hiding opportunities and access to appropriate temperatures.

If none of these factors are inappropriate -- and therefore likely to be causing the problem -- consult your veterinarian. Above all, do not panic – snakes can go very long periods of time without food. Your veterinarian will want to make sure that your snake is in good health, as respiratory infections or internal parasites may cause it to refuse food.

Some snakes refuse food in the winter, as would happen in the wild. While you should consult with your veterinarian the first time this happens, subsequent refusals during the winter do not usually indicate a problem.

Mouth rot, respiratory illness and parasites can cause snakes to refuse food.

Chapter 19: Selected Species Accounts

While all kingsnakes and milksnakes share some common characteristics, each form has at least a few unique characteristics. The following are some notes and information about a select few kingsnakes and milksnakes.

Eastern Kingsnakes (Lampropeltis getula)

Eastern kingsnakes are handsome and large snakes that often reach 4-feet in length; however, the largest ever recorded was nearly double that length – 82 inches (208 centimeters). They are dark brown or black snakes with a "chain link fence" pattern of yellow, cream or white lines on their backs and sides.

Eastern kingsnakes are not kept in captivity as often as some other kingsnakes, and this is unfortunate, as they are calm and easygoing captives.

While eastern kingsnakes are well-documented ophidiophages, they consume a wide variety of foods in the wild, and they are eager to do so in captivity as well. Most eastern kingsnakes are voracious eaters that will readily accept rodents when offered. They will also eat frogs, snakes, lizards and chicks, but a consistent diet of rodents suffices.

Wild-caught eastern kingsnakes often vibrate their tails, musk and adopt defensive postures – some even strike or bite. However, the majority settle down nicely once they are in captivity. Hatchlings may be nervous, but they quickly outgrow this.

Formerly considered the nominate subspecies of the common kingsnakes, most subspecies of the common kingsnake have been elevated to the rank of species (R. ALEXANDER PYRON1, 2009).

Some authorities consider the eastern kingsnakes inhabiting the outer banks of North Carolina to be a different subspecies – *Lampropeltis getula sticticeps*. These snakes often feature light colored, speckled scales and may be slightly larger. However, other authorities consider this population to be a regional variant, and undeserving of sub specific status.

Regardless of the taxonomic designation, the care of all the common kingsnakes is relatively similar.

Black Kingsnakes (Lampropeltis nigra)

Black kingsnakes are very similar to eastern kingsnakes, except that they usually stay a little smaller and have less pattern. The best examples of the species are almost completely black, but most show a few scattered light scales or the hint of a pattern. Hatchlings have bolder patterns than adults do, as the pattern tends to fade with age.

Black kingsnakes live in the southern United States, west of the range of the eastern kingsnake. They are habitat and prey generalists that may be found in forests, swampy areas, agricultural regions and suburban areas.

Black kingsnakes are not kept in captivity as often as other kingsnakes. Take care that you do not confuse black kingsnakes (*Lampropeltis nigra*) with desert black kingsnakes (*Lampropeltis nigritus*), which are more common in captive collections.

Speckled Kingsnakes (Lampropeltis holbrooki)

Speckled kingsnakes are attractive animals that feature a black ground color on top of which sits numerous bright yellow dots. Most of the snakes' dorsal scales feature a single, yellow dot. In some lighting, the combination of the dots and dark ground color give the overall impression of a green snake.

Most grow to lengths of 3- to 4- feet (90 to 120 centimeters), although they have been recorded as long as 5-feet (152 centimeters). Found west of the Mississippi river in the central

United States, speckled kings inhabit a variety of habitats, including forests, riparian areas and suburban regions.

Speckled kings are dietary generalists, which, like many other kingsnakes, eagerly consume virtually any small animal they encounter. This may include snakes, rodents and birds.

Most speckled kings become tame captives, but occasional specimens remain nervous and flighty for their entire lives.

Desert Kingsnakes (Lampropeltis splendida)

Desert kingsnakes are some of the most handsome members of the common kingsnake group. Most have a black ground color, which is topped with numerous yellow speckles. The pattern and distribution of the speckles is such that black blotches remain on top of the back, producing interesting "dotted line" pattern down the snakes' backs.

Desert kingsnakes range through central Mexico and encroach slightly into Nevada and Texas. Additionally, some individuals may occur in extreme east Arizona. Desert kingsnakes intergrade with speckled kingsnakes across the eastern portions of their range.

Desert kingsnakes are frequently kept in captivity and make excellent pets for novice keepers. An axanthic form is known, in which the animal produces no yellow pigments, and look like a black and white version of the species.

Mexican Black Kingsnake (Lampropeltis nigrita)

The Mexican black kingsnake is one of the most spectacular looking species of the genus. Jet-black from head to tail as adults, the young usually bear some faint pattern elements, which fade quickly with age.

Nocturnal in the wild, captives may be active at any time. However, like most of their relatives, Mexican black kingsnakes are generally shy and spend most of their time hiding. Nevertheless, they are usually calm and docile pets.

Constrictors of rodents, lizards and snakes in the wild, Mexican black kingsnakes adapt well to captivity and usually feed on rodents with few problems.

Mexican black kingsnakes are quite prolific, and may deposit clutches of up to 24 eggs.

California Kingsnakes (Lampropeltis californiae)

California kingsnakes are perhaps the most commonly kept *Lampropeltis* species in the world. It is easy to understand why – most are voracious eaters, they average between 3 and 4 feet in length (90 to 120 centimeters) and they are available in a variety of color and pattern morphs.

California kingsnakes are generalist predators that are as likely to hunt snakes, as they are lizards or rodents. This opportunistic attitude towards food acquisition benefits their keepers, who often find the snakes to be easy to feed.

Some California kingsnakes are very tame animals, while others remain skittish throughout their lives. It behooves new keepers to purchase yearlings, whose personality is better established than that of a hatchling. Even California kingsnakes that are not tame are not particularly likely to bite. However, as with all kingsnakes, bites are essentially harmless.

California kingsnakes naturally occur in several different color and pattern varieties. Many animals from the coast are brown with cream-colored bands, while those referred to as "desert phase" are jet black with white bands. In other locations, the animals possess a single vertebral stripe as opposed to bands. Still other areas feature snakes with blotched patterns. A kaleidoscope of possibilities awaits those who seek to keep a captive produced California kingsnake.

Gray-Banded Kingsnakes (Lampropeltis alterna)

Gray-banded kingsnakes are very popular species with hobbyists, and it is easy to see why. Clad in gorgeous colors and patterns, and possessing gentle temperaments, gray-banded kingsnakes are always favorites in any collection.

Interestingly, this species was originally thought to be two different species: *Lampropeltis alterna* and *Lampropeltis blairi*. However, once the species was bred in captivity, it became apparent that the snakes were actually the same species – they simply occur in two different color forms.

Both phases have gray ground color that varies from light to dark. On top of the gray color, the alterna-phase animals feature thin black and red bands. Blairi-phase animals have broad red or orange blotches on their backs.

Geographic factors affect the extent to which the morphs are found in different areas. The northeastern populations tend to produce more blairi morphs, whereas the southern portions of the range produce more alterna morphs.

Some researchers have suggested that gray-banded kingsnakes may be mimics. The alterna-phase animals strongly resemble banded rock rattlesnakes (*Crotalus lepidus klauberi*) while the blairi-phase animals resemble trans-Pecos (*Agkistrodon contortrix phaeogaster*) and broad-banded copperheads (*Agkistrodon contortrix laticinctus*). Gray-banded kingsnakes have rather distinct, triangular-shaped heads, which makes them resemble the venomous pit vipers even more.

If this mimicry hypothesis is correct, it explains why central Mexican alterna populations primarily produce alterna-phase animals, as no copperheads inhabit the area. It also suggests that mimicry may be even more widespread in the genus than commonly thought.

Unfortunately, given their considerable beauty, gray-banded kingsnakes are secretive, largely nocturnal, serpents. However, gray-banded kingsnakes are often very calm and they usually accept handling in stride.

Gray-banded kingsnakes live in arid, rocky habitats, where they primarily prey on lizards that they find while actively foraging at night. In captivity, this species can be reluctant to accept rodent prey as hatchlings, although many adults accept them eagerly.

Yearlings and well-started juveniles make excellent snakes for novice keepers.

Mexican Kingsnakes (Lampropeltis mexicana)

The taxonomy of many Mexican kingsnakes is poorly understood. This is due to several reasons, including socio-political instability, crime and narcoterrorism in the region. Virtually all animals in captivity are the progeny of captives from the United States, Canada or Europe.

While they thrive in experienced hands, they share the common challenges presented by many other kingsnakes: The young are very small and they prefer lizards for food. Additionally, relatively little is known about the natural history of these species and subspecies, making captive husbandry more difficult.

Accordingly, these are not ideal pets for novices, but success is possible with well-established juveniles or yearlings.

The taxonomy of this complex is in a state of constant flux. This is likely to continue until the area becomes safer to work in, and researchers can properly document the ranges of the various forms.

Previously, the species has been host to the gray-banded kingsnake, which was recognized as *Lampropeltis mexicana alterna*, and the Queretaro Mountain kingsnake, which is currently recognized as its own species by most authorities, who designate it *Lampropeltis ruthveni*.

While not recognized by all authorities, many recognize three different subspecies:

Mexican Kingsnakes (*Lampropeltis mexicana mexicana*)

Sometimes called "MexMex" by breeders and kingsnake enthusiasts, the nominate form of the species is thought to inhabit the center of the complex's range.

Mexican kingsnakes usually possess a gray ground color on top of which sit reddish-orange saddles.

Variable Kingsnakes (*Lampropeltis mexicana thayeri*)

Variable kingsnakes are a polymorphic species that occur in a variety of color forms. They are generally banded or covered in numerous saddles, but the thickness and shape of these markings varies widely. Their ground color ranges from straw-yellow to grey to orange, and the saddles can be nearly as many different colors, but red tones are the most common.

The primary three variations include banded, tricolored animals (milksnake phase), animals with numerous, usually narrow saddles (leonis phase) and rare examples that are all black.

Variable kings are very popular among breeders, as the possibilities of producing different "flavors" of eye-candy snakes are endless. Each clutch of eggs results in surprises. However, they share the same challenges as most of their close relatives, and beginners should purchase established animals rather than hatchlings.

Durango Mountain Kingsnakes (*Lampropeltis mexicana greeri*)

Durango Mountain kingsnakes are very similar to variable and Mexican kingsnakes. Usually, they have a grey-green ground color and orange or red saddles or markings. They appear somewhat similar to Mexican kingsnakes, with the primary difference being of the head coloration.

Milk Snakes (Lampropeltis triangulum spp.)

Milksnakes are some of the most attractive snakes that are available to hobbyists. While most authorities still consider them to be a single species, others have elevated many forms to the level of full species.

The variation in milksnakes is drastic. Ranging from Canada to Ecuador, the snakes vary greatly in size as well. (CISNEROS-HEREDIA, 2006) Many species are small, lizard eating species while others are the largest snakes in the genus.

Honduran Milksnakes (*Lampropeltis triangulum hondurensis*)

Honduran milksnakes are among the best kingsnakes for beginners to select. While they do attain very large sizes by kingsnake standards – some adults reach 6-feet (182 centimeters) in length or more – they are still manageable.

Honduran milksnakes are generally eager feeders and because they hatch at large sizes, they are able to eat relatively large prey for their first meal. While some insist on lizard-scented rodents, others eat unscented rodents with gusto.

Honduran milksnakes typically appear as large, red-white-and-black serpents. However, in captivity, a number of mutations have been produced. This has made "typical" or "wild type" Honduran milksnakes somewhat rare.

One of the most common mutations is the "tangerine" or "bicolor" phase. These animals usually have orange, rather than white, bands. Sometimes, the "orange" and "red" bands are very similar in color. This produces a two-color snake, with double black rings surrounding a reddish-orange body.

While hatchlings can be somewhat flighty and prone to musking on their keepers, adults are typically calm and docile. However, Honduran Milksnakes do have very strong feeding drives, so caution is necessary during feeding times.

Pueblan Milksnake (*Lampropeltis triangulum campbelli*)

Pueblan milksnakes are very popular among kingsnake enthusiasts, and they are one of the hardier forms available in the hobby. Pueblan milksnakes are a relatively small species, averaging slightly less than 36 inches (91 centimeters) in length.

Pueblan milksnakes are shy, but they are among the least likely kingsnakes to bite. Pueblans typically prefer to start feeding on lizards or lizard-scented prey, so beginners should seek established animals.

Pueblan milksnakes are available in several color variations.

Sinaloan Milksnakes (*Lampropeltis triangulum sinaloae*)

The Sinaloan Milksnake is a very attractive species that is a great choice for beginners. Sinaloan milksnakes were formerly considered a local form of the Nelson's milksnake (*Lampropeltis triangulum nelsoni*), but currently, they are treated as a distinct subspecies. (Applegate, n.d.)

One of the reddest milksnakes, Sinaloans have broad red rings, punctuated by relatively few, black and yellow triads. Sinaloans reach almost 4-feet (120 centimeters) in length, although most are somewhat smaller.

Sinaloan milksnakes are among the tamest milksnakes, and they are usually excellent eaters. The finest looking examples have little to no black "tipping" in their red or yellow bands.

Black Milksnakes (*Lampropeltis triangulum gaigeae*)

The black milksnake is one of the most interesting forms of the species. Inhabiting Costa Rica and Panama, the large milksnakes undergo a spectacular ontogenetic color change. As hatchlings, black milksnakes resemble most other milksnakes, and possess bold, red, black and yellow bands. However, as they grow, the snakes slowly turn black. As adults, they are stunning, jet-black animals.

Some researchers hypothesize that this color change is an adaptation for living in the high mountains. The cooler temperatures of high elevations make it more difficult for snakes to bask. When all other things are equal, it takes longer for a large snake to raise its core body temperature than it does for a small snake.

This means that the young may be able to achieve suitable body temperatures despite their bold colors, while the adults benefit from the increased amount of heat they absorb, courtesy of their black coloration.

This also makes sense in terms of predator avoidance. While the bright coral-snake-like colors may help the young to defend themselves, the adults, who have fewer predators, are able to survive without the mimicry. Additionally, the black color may provide better camouflage for the adults.

In captivity, black milksnakes are hardy captives that have rather docile personalities. They cost more than some more common forms, such as Pueblan milksnakes, but they make up for that with beauty, size and personality.

Eastern Milksnakes (*Lampropeltis triangulum triangulum*)

The eastern milksnake is not seen in captivity as much as some of the other forms, but it should not be overlooked. Attaining at least 4-feet (120 centimeters) in total length, these robust milksnakes have blotched or saddled color patterns, instead of the tricolored pattern so many of their relatives possess.

Scientists debate the reasons for the different colors of this subspecies. One possible explanation is that coral snakes are not found in the same range in most places as eastern milksnakes.

Eastern milksnakes are usually rather docile, although the hatchlings often vibrate their tails, flatten their heads and strike when frightened.

In the wild, eastern milksnakes feed on rodents, lizards and snakes, but they likely consume other creatures – specifically birds – when the opportunity arises. In captivity, they usually learn to accept rodents, although they may prefer lizard-scented prey initially.

Eastern milksnakes are found from southern Canada to north Georgia in the east, and as far west as Minnesota. They are replaced in the Deep South by the scarlet kingsnake (*Lampropeltis elapsoides*) and the Louisiana milksnake (*Lampropeltis triangulum amaura*) and in the central United States by the central plains milksnake (*Lampropeltis triangulum gentilis*) and the red milksnake (*Lampropeltis triangulum syspila*).

Along each of these borders, eastern milksnakes interbreed with their con specifics. Some authorities recognize a distinct race in the region of coastal North Carolina, thought to be a place where scarlet kingsnakes and eastern milksnakes interbreed.

Scarlet Kingsnakes (Lampropeltis elapsoides)

Scarlet kingsnakes are among the smallest of all the kingsnakes; in fact, they are some of the smallest of all the snakes commonly kept in captivity. The longest recorded scarlet kingsnake measured 27 inches (69 centimeters); but most are less than 20 inches (50 centimeters) long. Some are tiny, measuring little more than a 12 inches (30 centimeters) in length at maturity.

Scarlet kingsnakes are very secretive snakes that spend most of their time underground or under the bark of trees – particularly pine trees (*Pinus* sp.). Scarlet kingsnakes primarily inhabit the coastal plain of the southeastern United States.

These small kingsnakes subsist almost entirely on lizards in the wild. In captivity, it can be very difficult to transition them to a rodent diet. Some scarlet kingsnakes are defensive and nervous animals, while others are rather calm. As a whole, the species has a well-deserved reputation for being escape artists.

While scarlet kingsnakes are very attractive animals, clad in dark red, yellow and black rings, they are not commonly kept by hobbyists because of their food preferences. In the hands of experienced keepers, they may thrive, but, due to their small size and dietary preferences, scarlet kingsnakes are not recommended for beginners.

California Mountain Kingsnakes (*Lampropeltis zonata*)

California Mountain Kingsnakes are very attractive serpents, with fine, tri-colored banding. California Mountain kingsnakes can be distinguished from their similar-looking relatives, the Arizona Mountain kingsnakes (*Lampropeltis pyromelana*) by noting the snout color. Typically, California Mountain kingsnakes have black snouts, while the Arizona natives have white noses.

California mountain kingsnakes are secretive snakes that spend most of their time in rock piles. Rather than venturing out into the open to bask, most utilize the gradient afforded by the rock pile. For example, when a snake needs to elevate its body temperature, it moves towards the surface of the rock pile where temperatures are higher.

Hobbyists, breeders and researchers have historically divided this species into as many as seven subspecies. However, the most recent taxonomic work on the form recognized two distinct species. The northern species is considered *Lampropeltis zonata*, while the southern species is designated as *Lampropeltis multifasciata*. (Multilocus phylogeographic assessment of the California Mountain Kingsnake (*Lampropeltis zonata*) suggests alternative patterns of diversification for the California Floristic Province, 2013) The authors of the study did recognize that the southern form itself is composed of two different lineages.

California mountain kingsnakes inhabit high elevations. Most are found over 3,000 feet above sea level, but occasionally individuals have been found over 6,000 feet over sea level. At these high elevations, the local temperatures are slightly cool.

This is reflected in the captive care of these snakes, who prefer well-defined thermal gradients, ranging from 65 degrees Fahrenheit to 85 degrees Fahrenheit (18 to 29 degrees Celsius).

Most breeders cool their California mountain kingsnakes to the low 50s Fahrenheit (10 to 12 degrees Celsius) for three months or longer. Adults usually respond very aggressively to food after exiting brumation and begin breeding soon. Eggs hatch between 50 and 65 days when incubated in the low 80s Fahrenheit (26 to 28 degrees Celsius). Clutches may include up to 10 eggs, but the average is approximately 7.

Hatchling California mountain kingsnakes strongly prefer lizards to rodents, and often require scent-transfer techniques. Adults reach about 3-feet (91 centimeters) in length, but are slender and require relatively small mice for food.

In the wild, California mountain kingsnakes prey primarily on lizards, although rodents, reptile eggs and birds have also been recorded as prey. California mountain kingsnake prey averages average about one-third of the snake's mass (RODRIGUEZ-ROBLES, Feeding Ecology of the California Mountain Kingsnake, Lampropeltis zonata (Colubridae), 2003).

One California mountain kingsnake lived for more than 26 years in captivity.

Arizona Mountain Kingsnakes (Lampropeltis pyromelana)

Like the California mountain kingsnake (*Lampropeltis zonata*), the Arizona mountain kingsnake lives at high elevations. Found between 3,000 and 7,000 feet above sea level, these diurnal snakes are adapted to slightly cooler temperatures, as their California mountain kingsnake relatives are.

Breeding commences after a three-month brumation period of about 50 degrees Fahrenheit (10 degrees Celsius). Arizona mountain kingsnake eggs hatch in about 60 days, when incubated at about 82 degrees Fahrenheit (27 degrees Celsius).

Rodents and lizards are the primary prey of these rock-dwelling snakes. Often, Arizona mountain kingsnakes inhabit rock piles located near wooded streams. Arizona mountain kings likely remain close to their rock piles for most of their lives.

Unlike most kingsnakes that do not climb often, many Arizona mountain kingsnakes have been observed climbing in bushes and trees up to 6 feet (182 centimeters) high. It is possible that such snakes are foraging for nestling birds.

Prairie Kingsnake (Lampropeltis calligaster)

Prairie kingsnakes (also called yellow-bellied kingsnakes) are handsome brown snakes that reach about 48 inches (120 centimeters) in length. While they lack the bold colors of some of their relatives, prairie kings often make up for this with their pleasant personalities. Often, prairie kingsnakes are quite docile and more relaxed than high-strung forms, such as California kingsnakes (*Lampropeltis californiae*).

One of the drawbacks of prairie kingsnakes is that they are quite secretive – even by kingsnake standards. A 2006 study, published in the "Journal of Herpetology," noted that radio tracked prairie kingsnakes often spent as much as 73 percent of their time underground (Matthew L. Richardson, 2006). Some individuals spent two-week long stretches below the surface. When the snakes do travel to the surface, they rarely do so during the day (MATTHEW L. RICHARDSON, 2006).

This means that your pet will spend the vast majority of his time hiding. Nevertheless, prairie kings are popular because of the ease with which they can be cared for and their gentle personalities.

Breeders have established amelanistic (albino) and striped forms in captivity, which has added to their popularity. Prairie kings are relatively easy to breed in captivity. They require a three-month period of brumation with temperatures in the mid-50s Fahrenheit (approximately 12 degrees Celsius). The adults should be fed well after emerging from dormancy, and pairings can begin a week or two later.

The females deposit up to 15 eggs, one to two months later. When incubated between 78 and 82 degrees Fahrenheit (25 to 27 degrees Celsius), the young hatch in about 45 to 60 days.

The prairie king's close relatives, the mole kings (*Lampropeltis calligaster rhombomaculata*) also make suitable captives, but they are not as common in captivity. The South Florida mole king (*Lampropeltis calligaster occipitolineata*) is also similar, but is protected and rarely seen in captivity.

Additional Resources

Never stop learning more about your new pet's natural history and biology of captive care. Doing so will allow you to provide your new pet with the highest level of care possible.

Books

Kingsnakes and Milksnakes: Everything about Purchase, Housing, Health Care, and Breeding

Richard D. Bartlett, Ronald G. Markel

Barron's Educational Series

The General Care and Maintenance of Common Kingsnakes

David Perlowin

BowTie Inc.,

Alterna: The Gray Banded Kingsnake

Gerold Merker, Walter Merker

Lm Digital,

King Snake

Burke Davis

Scholastic

Kingsnakes and Milk Snakes

Ronald G. Markel, Richard D. Bartlett

Barron's Educational Series,

Zonata: The California Mountain Kingsnake

143

Mitchell Mulks

Lm Digital

Snakes: Their Care and Keeping

Lenny Flank

Howell Book House

Keeping Snakes: A Practical Guide to Caring for Unusual Pets

David Manning

Barron's Educational Series

The Art of Keeping Snakes: From the Experts at Advanced Vivarium Systems

Philippe De Vosjoli

Advanced Vivarium Systems

Snakes: Everything about Selection, Care, Nutrition, Diseases, Breeding, and Behavior

Richard D. Bartlett, Patricia Pope Bartlett

Barron's Educational Series

Snakes of the Southeast

J. Whitfield Gibbons, Michael E. Dorcas

University of Georgia Press

Milksnakes and Tricolored Kingsnakes

Richard D. Bartlett, Patricia Bartlett

Barron's Educational Series

Milk Snakes

W. P. Mara

TFH Publications Incorporated

Milksnakes

Bryan Engler

BowTie Press

The General Care and Maintenance of Milk Snakes

Robert Applegate

Advanced Vivarium Systems

Infectious Diseases and Pathology of Reptiles: Color Atlas and Text (Google eBook)

Elliott Jacobson

CRC Press

What's Wrong with My Snake?

John Rossi, Roxanne Rossi

BowTie Press

Magazines

Reptiles Magazine

www.reptilesmagazine.com/

Covering reptiles commonly kept in captivity, kingsnakes are frequently featured in the magazine, and its online partner.

Practical Reptile Keeping

http://www.practicalreptilekeeping.co.uk/

Practical Reptile Keeping is a popular publication aimed at beginning and advanced hobbies. Topics include the care and maintenance of popular reptiles as well as information on wild reptiles.

Websites

The Reptile Report

www.thereptilereport.com/

The Reptile Report is a news-aggregating website that accumulates interesting stories and features about reptiles from around the world.

Kingsnake.com

www.kingsnake.com

Started as a small website for gray-banded kingsnake enthusiasts, Kingsnake.com has become one of the largest reptile-oriented portals in the hobby. Includes classifieds, breeder directories, message forums and other resources.

The Vivarium and Aquarium News

www.vivariumnews.com/

The online version of the former publication, The Vivarium and Aquarium News provides in-depth coverage of different reptiles and amphibians in a captive and wild context.

Applegate Reptiles

www.applegatereptiles.com

Robert Applegate has over 50 years' experience breeding kingsnakes and milksnakes. His website contains animals for sale as well as numerous informational pages.

Sierra Herps

www.sierraherps.com

Sierra Herps produces mexicana-group Lampropeltis. Additionally, their website contains a plethora of resources.

Arizona-Sonora Desert Museum

www.ssarherps.org/

The Arizona-Sonora Desert Museum provides information and educational resources about all things desert-related. The site contains ample information about some of the kingsnakes that live in the desert.

Amphibians and Reptiles of North Carolina

http://www.herpsofnc.org/

Published and maintained by Davidson College, this website details the various reptiles and amphibians that inhabit North Carolina. Information is provided for Eastern kingsnakes, scarlet kingsnakes and eastern milksnakes.

Florida Museum of Natural History

www.flmnh.ufl.edu/

A division of the University of Florida, the Florida Museum of Natural History website provides a wealth of information on the snakes that call Florida home. Specifically, the website provides information on Eastern and Florida kingsnakes, as well as scarlet kingsnakes.

Savannah River Ecology Laboratory

http://srel.uga.edu/

A division of the University of Georgia, Athens, the Savannah River Ecology Laboratory conducts research and publishes educational information about the reptiles and amphibians of Georgia and South Carolina.

Journals

Herpetologica

www.hljournals.org/

Published by The Herpetologists' League, Herpetologica, and its companion publication, Herpetological Monographs cover all aspects of reptile and amphibian research.

Journal of Herpetology

www.ssarherps.org/

Produced by the Society for the Study of Reptiles and Amphibians, the Journal of Herpetology is a peer-reviewed publication covering a variety of reptile-related topics.

Copeia

www.asihcopeiaonline.org/

Copeia is published by the American Society of Icthyologists and Herpetologists. A peer-reviewed journal, Copeia covers all aspects of the biology of reptiles, amphibians and fish.

Nature

www.nature.com/

Although Nature covers all aspects of the natural world, there is plenty for snake enthusiasts.

References

Applegate, R. (n.d.). *Nelson's Milksnakes*. Retrieved from http://www.applegatereptiles.com/: http://www.applegatereptiles.com/species/nelsoni.htm

CHRISTOPHER T. WINNE, J. D. (2007). Enigmatic Decline of a Protected Population of Eastern Kingsnakes, Lampropeltis getula, in South Carolina. *COPEIA*.

CISNEROS-HEREDIA, D. F. (2006). On the distribution and conservation of Lampropeltis triangulum (LACÉPÈDE, 1789) in Ecuador. *HERPETOZOA*.

David A. Steen1, 2. J. (2010). Multiscale Habitat Selection and Refuge Use of Common Kingsnakes, Lampropeltis getula, in Southwestern Georgia. *Copeia*.

David W. Kikuchi, D. W. (2006). High-model abundance may permit the gradual evolution of Batesian mimicry: an experimental test. *Royal Society Publishing*.

Fleet, H. S. (1970). Natural History of the Milk Snake (Lampropeltis triangulum) in Northeastern Kansas. *Herpetologica*.

Florida Museum of Natural History. (n.d.). *Eastern Kingsnake*. Retrieved from Florida Museum of Natural History: https://www.flmnh.ufl.edu/herpetology/fl-guide/Lampropeltisggetula.htm

KRYSKO1, K. L. (1995). Seasonal Activity of the Florida Kingsnake Lampropeltis getula floridana (Serpentes: Colubridae) in Southern Florida. *American Midland Naturalist*.

Matthew L. Richardson, 1. P. (2006). Habitat Use and Activity of Prairie Kingsnakesin Illinois. *Journal of Herpetology*.

MATTHEW L. RICHARDSON, M. L. (2006). Habitat Use and Activity of Prairie Kingsnakes (Lampropeltis calligaster calligaster) in Illinois. *Journal of Herpetology*.

Multilocus phylogeographic assessment of the California Mountain Kingsnake (Lampropeltis zonata) suggests alternative patterns of diversification for the California Floristic Province. (2013). *Molecular Ecology*.

R. ALEXANDER PYRON1, 3. &. (2009). Systematics of the Common Kingsnake (Lampropeltis getula; Serpentes: Colubridae) and the burden of heritage in taxonomy. *Zootaxa*.

R. G. Zweifel, H. C. (1983). Multiple insemination demonstrated experimentally in the kingsnake (Lampropeltis getulus). *Experientia*.

RODRIGUEZ-ROBLES, H. W. (2003). Feeding Ecology of the California Mountain Kingsnake, Lampropeltis zonata (Colubridae). *Copeia*.

RODRIGUEZ-ROBLES, H. W. (2003). Feeding Ecology of the California Mountain Kingsnake, Lampropeltis zonata (Colubridae). *Copeia*.

Published by IMB Publishing 2014

CPSIA information can be obtained
at www.ICGtesting.com
Printed in the USA
LVOW01s0128310516

490493LV00010B/30/P